D1490032

KNITTING

HEARTLAND

ACKNOWLEDGEMENTS
Text & photographs
Copyright © 2001 Jo Sharp Pty Ltd
ISBN 0-9587033-5-3
All rights reserved.
No portion of this book may be
reproduced mechanically,
electronically or by any other means,
including photocopying,
without written permission.
Published in 2001 by Jo Sharp Pty Ltd

Printed in Western Australia.
Printing, Frank Daniels
Pre-Press, CDC Graphics
Photography & Book Design, Jo Sharp
Graphic design assistance, Bronia Richards
Computer wizz, Scott Parsons

Knitwear Design
Jo Sharp, Leanne Prouse, Wendy Richards

Knitting
Norma Beard, Janet Best, Wendy Carmen
Lily Deroost, Francesca Greaves,
Jenny Green, Betty Hawkins,
Gwen Howson, Marilyn Theisel,
Kathleen Waldron,
Whitney Weaver, Dot Lamley,
Leanne Prouse, Coby Yzerman.

Photography Assistance
Andrew Markovs, Wendy Richards,
Leanne Prouse.

Location credits
Thanks for the assistance we received
at the homestead's of
Margaret & Mary, Anne & Dom,
Margaret & Athol, Lorraine & Rob,
Cheryl & Rod.
Thanks also to Matt & Kylie for
their assistance with the horses.
Special thanks to Kate
at Madison Hall
Children's Wear store in Albany
for all co-ordinates.

Models
Thank you to all our talented young models
Leteesha, Phoebe, Imogen, Edwina
Johnathan, Lilly, Rachel, Ashlinn,
Geordie, Tess, Fergus, Budgie, Marina,
Anthony, Brandon, Ella, Anna
...and of course
a big thanks to all the patient
and helpful parents who
accompanied their children
on our photo shoots.

Thanks to Rodney the rooster,
Blue the dog, Bronte the horse
and Olympia the goat,
who lives on in this book.

Blossom Cap
Pattern on page 45

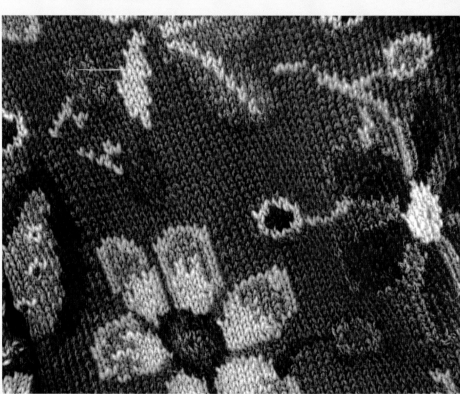

INTRODUCTION

When I knit life slows down to a pace that makes sense. Between the stitches there is time to unravel my day. Knitting creates an environment for beauty to happen. The idea of working with coloured woollen yarn, of working stitches to create fabric, brings to me an acute awareness of life's possibilities.

A book of children's knits I could resist no longer! Working with colour and stitch variations to create fabric ideas for this book was too much fun! Once the book was begun, it was only a matter of weeks before the studio was abuzz with the excitement of a new collection taking shape. Being children's knits, samples were completed very quickly, which inspired us to create more...and more.....until we came to the conclusion that a second children's knitwear book would be necessary to accommodate all of our ideas!

Designing knitwear for children, brought to this project unlimited scope for excursions into colour, busy surface design and crocheted or knitted embellishments.

In this book, as in my other books, I have included a good number of patterns that are practical and easy to knit for beginners. There are also wildly complex surface designs and cabled knits for those who enjoy a greater degree of challenge in their work.

I do believe, more than ever, that knitting is the ideal antidote to today's frenetic, computer tapping, email zapping environment. In the 21st century where everything we encounter is push button or instantaneous, knitting takes thought, requires manual dexterity and allows time for reflection.

I dedicate this book to the continuation of the nourishing and enriching craft of hand knitting. A craft relevant to individuals from all walks of life today.

Jo Sharp

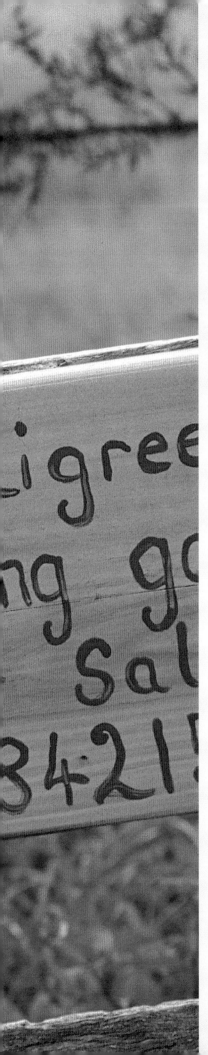

Lucy Lou
Version 1
Pattern on page 34

Laurie
Version 1
Pattern on page 12

Those goats were here

a minute ago...

Sasha's scarf
Version 2
Pattern on page 48
Heartland (sweater)
Version 1
Pattern on page 5
Tilly Dolls
Versions 1 & 2
Patterns on page 21

Left
Poppy Version 1
Pattern on page 37
Right
Matilda, version 1
Pattern on page 40

Amelia, Version 1
Pattern on page 30

Matilda, Version 2
Pattern on page 40

Liza, Version 2
Pattern on page 24

Leonora, (vest) Version 1
Pattern on page 36
Matilda, (sweater) Version 3
Pattern on page 40

This page
Phoebe's Bag, Version 1
Pattern on page 44

Matilda (sweater) Version 3
Pattern on page 40

Opposite page
Hawthorn, Version 3
Pattern on page 8

This page
Sasha's Scarf, version 1
Pattern on page 48
Lucy Lou (sweater) version 5
Pattern on page 34

Opposite page
Phoebe's Bag, version 2
Pattern on page 44
Lucy Lou (sweater) version 4
Pattern on page 34

Underneath the almond tree,

... is a very good place to be.

This page
Annabel (skirt)
Version 2
Pattern on page 28
Lucy Lou (sweater)
Version 3
Pattern on page 34
Opposite page
Top left
My Favourite Scarf
Version 3
Pattern on page 14
Top right & bottom
Amelia, Versions 2 & 3
Patterns on page 30

Liza, Version 1
Pattern on page 24

This page & opposite
Eloise
Versions 1 & 2
Patterns on page 16

Heartland, Version 2
Pattern on page 5

Truly Timeless (sweaters)
Versions 1 & 2
Patterns on page 17
Navy Beanie
Pattern on page 47

Moss Stitch Beanie,
Version 1
Pattern on page 47

This is how it was at grandad's place
with his clever dog, "Blue".

This page, boy
Harper (sweater)
Version 1, pattern on page 19
My Favourite Scarf
Version 1, pattern on page 14

This page and page opposite, girl
Hawthorne, Version 1
Pattern on page 8

Truly Timeless, Version 1
Pattern on page 17

Opposite page
Hawthorn, Version 1
Pattern on page 8

Leonora (vest) version 2
Pattern on page 36
Lucy Lou (sweater) version 3
Pattern on page 34

Truly Timeles
Version
pattern on page 1

Heartland, Version 3
Pattern on page 5

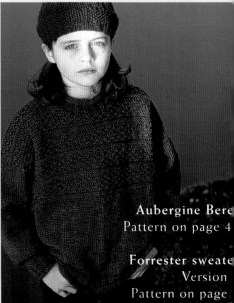

Aubergine Bere
Pattern on page 4

Forrester sweate
Version
Pattern on page

Heartland, (sweater)
Version 2
Pattern on page 5

My Favourite Scarf
Version 2
Pattern on page 14

This page
Lucy Lou, Version 2
Pattern on page 34
Moss Stitch Beanie, Version 2
Pattern on page 47

Right
Sienne, Version 2
Pattern on page 22

Home is ...
where the heart is

This Page & opp. top
Poppy, Version 2
Pattern on page 37
Opposite Page,
Bottom right, Sienne,
Version 2
Pattern on page 22
Bottom left
Lucy Lou (sweater)
Version 2
Pattern on page 34
& Moss Stitch Beanie,
Version 2,
Pattern on page 47

This Page
Sienne, Version 2
Pattern on page 22

Opposite Page
Harper, Version 3
Pattern on page 19

This Page,
Laurie, Version 2
Pattern on page 12

Opposite Page, Far left
Hawthorn, Version 2
Pattern on page 8

This Page
Laurie, Version 2
Pattern on page 12

Opposite Page
Hawthorn, Version 2
Pattern on page 8

This Page, front
Harper, Version 2
Pattern on page 19
This Page, behind
Sienne, Version 1
Pattern on page 22
Opposite Page
Sienne, Version 1
Pattern on page 22

This Page, left
Heartland, Version 1
Pattern on page 5
Right
Forrester, Version 2
Pattern on page 3
Opposite Page, left
Heartland, Version 1
Pattern on page 5
Right
Harper, Version 4
Pattern on page 19

Another successful day
on the marsh...

See previous page for garment identification

JO SHARP

HAND KNITTING COLLECTION
8 PLY DK PURE WOOL HAND KNITTING YARN

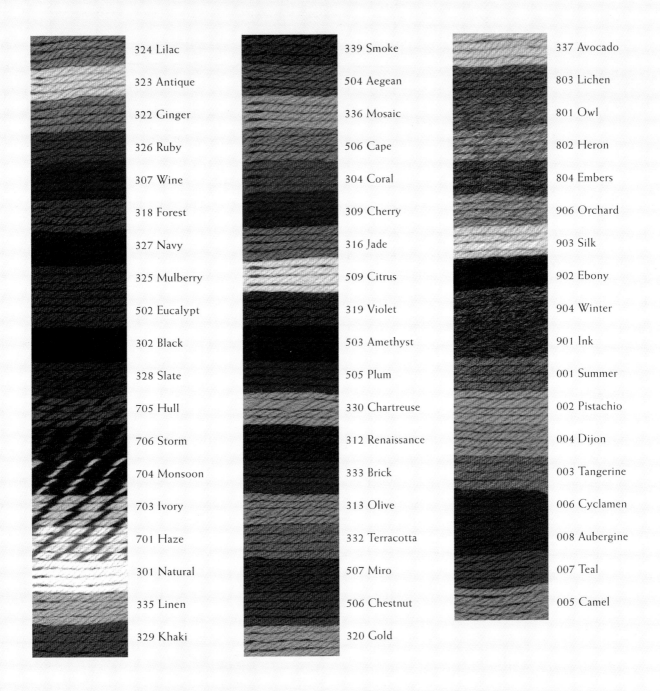

324 Lilac	339 Smoke	337 Avocado
323 Antique	504 Aegean	803 Lichen
322 Ginger	336 Mosaic	801 Owl
326 Ruby	506 Cape	802 Heron
307 Wine	304 Coral	804 Embers
318 Forest	309 Cherry	906 Orchard
327 Navy	316 Jade	903 Silk
325 Mulberry	509 Citrus	902 Ebony
502 Eucalypt	319 Violet	904 Winter
302 Black	503 Amethyst	901 Ink
328 Slate	505 Plum	001 Summer
705 Hull	330 Chartreuse	002 Pistachio
706 Storm	312 Renaissance	004 Dijon
704 Monsoon	333 Brick	003 Tangerine
703 Ivory	313 Olive	006 Cyclamen
701 Haze	332 Terracotta	008 Aubergine
301 Natural	507 Miro	007 Teal
335 Linen	506 Chestnut	005 Camel
329 Khaki	320 Gold	

Refer to page 52 for
information about the care
of Jo Sharp yarn.

Heartland (sweater)
Version 2
Pattern on page 5

My Favourite Scarf
Version 1
Pattern on page 14

KNITTING ABBREVIATIONS

alt	alternate
beg	beginning
cn	cable needle
col	colour
cm	centimetres
cont	continue
dec	decrease
foll	follow/ing
in	inch/es
inc	increase
incl.	including
K,k	knit
Kb1	Knit into the back of stitch
Kfb	Increase by knitting into front and back of K stitch.
m1	Make 1. Pick up loop between sts and knit into back of it.
mm	millimetres
patt	pattern
P,p	purl
Pbf	Increase by purling into back and front of P stitch.
psso	pass slip stitch over
rem	remain/ing
rep	repeat
rev	reverse/ing
RS	right side
skpsso	sl1, k1, psso.
sl	slip
st/s	stitch/es
st st	Stocking Stitch
tbl	through back of loop
tog	together
WS	wrong side
yb	yarn back
yf	yarn forward
yrn	yarn round needle

CROCHET ABBREVIATIONS

Ch	chain
dc	double crochet
htr	half treble
dbl	double treble
tr	treble
sl st	slip stitch

CONTENTS

Contents, Knitting & Crochet Abbreviations . . .1

General Pattern Instructions 2

Forrester .3

Heartland .5

Hawthorn .8

Laurie 12

My Favourite Scarf 14

Eloise 16

Truly Timeless 17

Harper 19

Tilly Doll 21

Sienne 22

Liza 24

Annabel .28

Amelia 30

Lucy Lou .34

Leonora .36

Poppy 37

Matilda .40

Phoebe's Bag 44

Blossom Cap 45

Aubergine Beret 46

Moss Stitch Beanie 47

Navy Beanie 47

Sasha's Scarf 48

Jo Sharp Yarn Stockists . . . . .49 - 51

How to Care for your Garment 52

GENERAL PATTERN INSTRUCTIONS

TENSION
At the start of each pattern, the required tension is given. Before beginning, it is most important that you knit a tension square. Using the stitch and needles specified in pattern, cast on 40 sts and knit approx. 40 rows. Lay work flat and without stretching, measure 10cm both vertically and horizontally with a ruler. Mark with pins. Count the stitches and rows between the pins which should match the required tension. If not, change your needle size. Note that smaller needles will bring the stitches closer together, larger needles will spread the stitches out. Incorrect tension will result in a mis-shapen garment. The use of a substitute yarn may also cause a mis-shapen garment.

If **stitch** tension is correct, but you are unable to achieve the correct **row** tension, you may need to work a different number of rows to those specified in the pattern to achieve the correct garment length.

SIZES
To ascertain which size garment to knit, use as a guide, a favourite old sweater which fits the intended wearer well. Compare the measurements of this garment with the measurements given in the pattern and choose the pattern size which most closely matches the existing garment.

READING GRAPHS
Each square on a graph represents one stitch. Unless otherwise stated, graphs are worked in Stocking Stitch. When working from a graph, read odd rows (RS) from right to left and even rows (WS) from left to right. Each colour is represented on the graph by a symbol. The colour key for symbols are given with each pattern. Graphs may be photocopy enlarged for easier reading.

YARN QUANTITIES
Yarn quantities given for garments are approximate estimations based on average requirements using specified tension and Jo Sharp 8ply DK Pure Wool Hand Knitting Yarn.

BUTTONHOLES
2 Stitch Buttonhole
Row 1 (RS) Work to buttonhole position, cast off 2 sts, work to end (or to next buttonhole).
Row 2 (WS) Work to buttonhole, cast on 2 sts in place of those cast off on previous row.

COLOUR REPRODUCTION
Inaccuracies of some illustrated yarn shades in this book are caused by photographic and printing reproduction processes and are unavoidable. To avoid disappointment, it is advisable to refer to a Jo Sharp Yarn Sample Card to view actual yarn shades specified in patterns before purchasing yarn.

KNITTING JO SHARP GARMENTS FOR RE-SALE
The knitting of garments from this book for re-sale is not permitted unless written consent is given from Jo Sharp Pty. Ltd.

PATTERN QUERIES
Jo Sharp Hand Knitting Yarns
PO Box 357,
Albany, WA 6331
Australia

Phone: +61 (08) 9842 2250
Fax: +61 (08) 9842 2260
Email: yarn@josharp.com.au
Website: www.josharp.com.au

FORRESTER

This textured gansey is sized for boys or girls and is a suitable project for a **beginner knitter**.

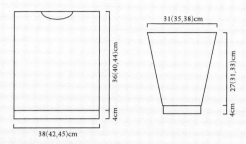

Version 1

Version 2

YARN

Jo Sharp 8 ply DK Pure Wool
Hand Knitting Yarn.

Colour	Quantity x 50g balls		
Version 1	3-4	(5-6	7-8)
Forest 318	8	9	10
Version 2	3-4	(5-6	7-8)
Eucalypt 502	8	9	10

MEASUREMENTS

(Measurements given in inches are approximate)
Unisex sizing

3-4	(5-6	7-8)	
To fit chest			
57 - 61	62 - 66	67 - 71	cm
22¹/₂ - 24	24¹/₂ - 26	26¹/₄ - 28	in
Bodice circumference			
74	82	88	cm
29¹/₄	32¹/₄	34³/₄	in
Bodice length			
40	44	48	cm
15³/₄	17¹/₄	19	in
Sleeve length			
31	35	37	cm
12¹/₄	13³/₄	14¹/₂	in

NEEDLES

1 pair 3.25mm needles (USA 3) (UK 10)
1 pair 3.75mm needles (USA 5) (UK 9)
1 pair 4.00mm needles (USA 6) (UK 8)
1 set 3.75mm circular needles (USA 5) (UK 9)

TENSION

22.5sts and 30 rows measured over 10cm
(approx. 4") st st using 4.00mm needles.

FRONT

Using 3.25mm needles, cast on 86(94,102)sts.
Work 6 rows Garter st (knit all rows).
Next row Purl.
Next row (RS) *K2, p2; rep from * to last 2 sts, k2.
Next row (WS) P2, * k2, p2, rep from * to end.
Repeat last 2 rows, 3 times (8 rows rib).
Change to 4.00mm needles.
Work 50(60,60)rows in st st.
Now refer to graph and continue on rep until front (incl. band) measures 34(38,42)cm, ending on a WS row.
Shape neck (RS) Patt 38(42,46)sts, turn, leave rem 48(52,56)sts on a holder. Keeping patt correct, cast off 3sts at neck edge on next row, then 2sts on foll alt rows, 4 times [27(31,35)sts] [9 shaping rows].
Work 8 rows without shaping. Cast off.
Place 10 centre sts on holder. Work second side to match first side, rev all shaping.

Forrester, continued...

BACK

Work back bodice to match front bodice, omitting front neck shaping and working back neck shaping into last 6 rows as follows;
(RS) Work 43(47,51)sts, turn, leave rem 43(47,51)sts on a holder. Cast off 5sts at beg next and foll alt row, then 6sts on foll alt row once, work to end of row. Cast off rem 27(31,35)sts. With RS facing, rejoin yarn to rem sts and work second side to match first side, rev all shaping.

SLEEVES

Using 3.75mm needles, cast on 34(38,42)sts. Work 2cm in st st, ending on a WS row. Now work 3cm in k2, p2 rib, ending on a WS row [34(38,42)sts]. Change to 4.00mm needles. **Shape sleeve** Now work in st st, inc 1st each end every 4th row, 18(12,12) times, then every foll 5th row, 0(8,10) times [70(78,86)sts] [72(88,98) shaping rows]. Work 8(6,2)rows staight. Cast off.

MAKING UP

Press all pieces gently on WS, using a warm iron over a damp cloth. Using Backstitch, join shoulder seams. Centre sleeves and join. Join side and sleeve seams, using Edge to Edge stitch on cuffs and bands. **Neckband** Using a 3.75mm circular needle, with RS facing, pick up and knit 23sts down left side front neck, 10 sts from stitch holder at centre front, 23sts up right side front neck and 32 sts across back neck (88sts). Work in k2, p2 rib for 9 rounds, then knit 6 rounds (st st). Cast off. Press seams.

FORRESTER, Bodice Graph

☐ K on RS, P on WS
■ P on RS, K on WS

HEARTLAND

This handsome, unisex, lightly cabled sweater with drop shoulder shaping is a suitable project for an **average skilled knitter**.

Version 1   Version 2   Version 3

YARN

Jo Sharp 8 ply DK Pure Wool
Hand Knitting Yarn.

Colour	Quantity x 50g balls		
Version 1	5-6	(7-8	9-10)
Tangerine 003	10	11	12
Version 2	5-6	(7-8	9-10)
Silk 903	10	11	12
Version 3	5-6	(7-8	9-10)
Ink 901	10	11	12

NEEDLES

1 pair 3.75mm needles (USA 5) (UK 9)
1 pair 4.00mm needles (USA 6) (UK 8)
1 set 4.00mm circular needles (USA 6) (UK 8)
1 cable needle

TENSION

22.5sts and 30 rows measured over 10cm
(approx. 4") st st using 4.00mm needles.

MEASUREMENTS

(Measurements given in inches are approximate)
Unisex sizing

5-6	(7-8	9-10)	
To fit chest			
62 - 66	67 - 71	72 - 76	cm
24¹/₂ - 26	26¹/₄ - 28	28¹/₄ - 30	in
Bodice circumference			
86	96	104	cm
33³/₄	37³/₄	41	in
Bodice length			
45	49	53	cm
17³/₄	19¹/₄	21	in
Sleeve length			
34.5	37	40.5	cm
13¹/₂	14¹/₂	16	in

44(49,53)cm   42.5(46.5,50.5)cm   2.5cm   34(38,40)cm   32(34.5,38)cm   2.5cm

Heartland, continued...

FRONT

Using 3.75mm needles, cast on
100(110,120)sts. Work 2.5cm in k1,p1
rib, ending on a WS row. Change to
4.00mm needles. Refer to Bodice Graph
A, work in pattern repeat until bodice
length (incl. band) measures
39(43,47)cm, ending on a WS row.
Shape neck Work 42(47,52)sts, turn
and leave rem sts on a holder.
Work each side of neck separately.
Cast off 3sts at beg of next row, then
3sts at neck edge on foll alt rows, 3
times [30(35,40)sts] (8 shaping rows).
Work 10 rows straight. Cast off.
With RS facing, leave 16 sts on a holder,
rejoin yarn to rem sts and complete
second side to match first side, rev all
shaping.

BACK

Work as for front, omitting neck
shaping.

SLEEVES

Using 3.75mm needles, cast on
39(43,45)sts. Work in k1,p1 rib for
2.5cm ending on a RS row. Inc 2 sts
evenly across next row [41(45,47)sts].
Change to 4.00mm needles.
Shape sleeve Working from Sleeve
Graph B, inc 1st each end of every 5th
row 18(20,22)times [77(85,91)sts]
[90(100,110)shaping rows].
Work 6(4,4)rows straight. Cast off.

MAKING UP

Press all pieces gently with a warm iron
over a damp cloth. Join shoulder seams.
Centre sleeves and join, join side and
sleeve seams.
Neckband With RS facing, using
4.00mm circular needle, pick up and knit
22sts down left front, 16sts from holder,
22sts up right front, 40sts across back
neck (100sts). Working in rounds of
k2,p2 rib, work until band measures 8cm.
Cast off in rib. Press seams.

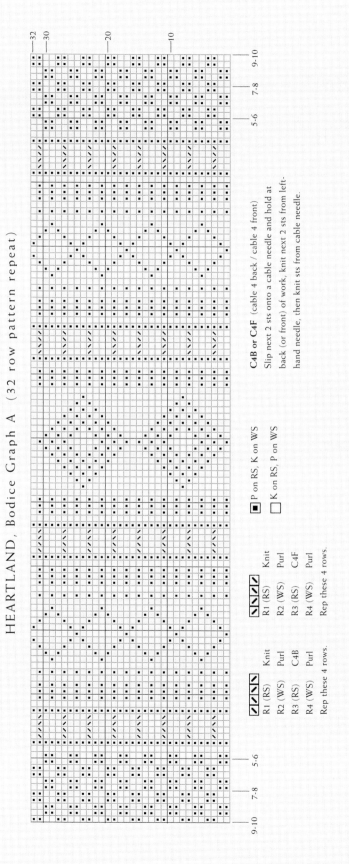

HEARTLAND, Bodice Graph A (32 row pattern repeat)

C4B or C4F (cable 4 back / cable 4 front)
Slip next 2 sts onto a cable needle and hold at
back (or front) of work, knit next 2 sts from left-
hand needle, then knit sts from cable needle.

■ P on RS, K on WS
□ K on RS, P on WS

			Knit
R1 (RS)	Purl
R2 (WS)	C4F
R3 (RS)	Purl
R4 (WS)	Rep these 4 rows.

			Knit
R1 (RS)	Purl
R2 (WS)	C4B
R3 (RS)	Purl
R4 (WS)	Rep these 4 rows.

HEARTLAND, Sleeve Graph B

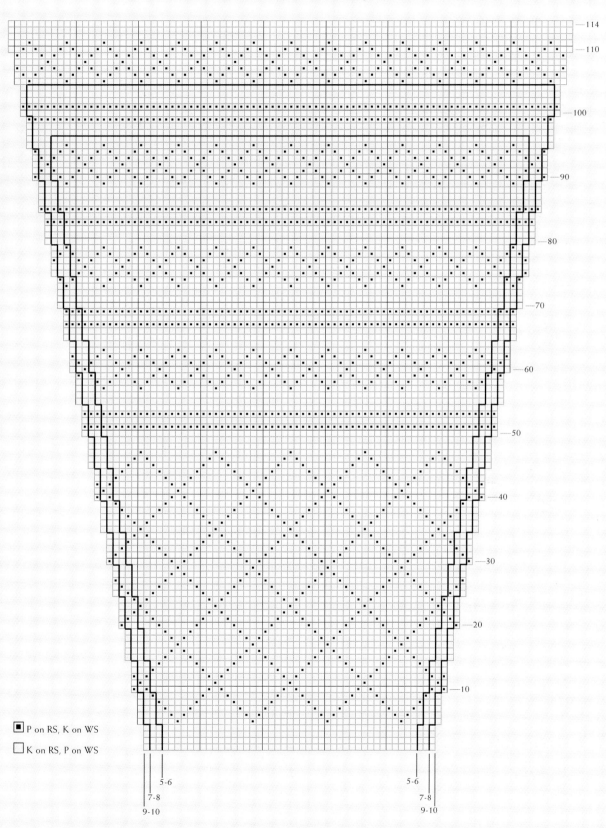

—114
—110
—100
—90
—80
—70
—60
—50
—40
—30
—20
—10

■ P on RS, K on WS

□ K on RS, P on WS

5-6

7-8

9-10

5-6

7-8

9-10

HAWTHORN

This sweater has drop shoulder shaping with a variety of band finishes and versions with either patterning on the bodice & sleeve or bodice only. A maximum of two colours are used in any single Fairisle row. This pattern is suitable for an **average skilled knitter** with **Fairisle** experience.

Version 1

Version 2

Version 3

YARN
Jo Sharp 8 ply DK Pure Wool
Hand Knitting Yarn.

Colour	Quantity x 50g balls		
Version 1	5-6	(7-8	9-10)
Navy 327	7	8	8
Forest 318	1	2	2
Aubergine 008	1	2	2
Orchard 906	1	1	1
Cyclamen 006	1	1	1
Mosaic 336	1	1	1
Version 2	5-6	(7-8	9-10)
Khaki 329	1	1	1
Slate 328	5	6	6
Antique 323	1	1	1
Heron 802	1	1	1
Chestnut 506	1	1	1
Gold 320	1	1	1
Version 3	5-6	(7-8	9-10)
Silk 903	8	9	9
Owl 801	1	1	1
Teal 007	1	1	1
Aubergine 008	1	1	1
Heron 802	1	1	1

MEASUREMENTS
(Measurements given in inches are approximate)
Unisex sizing

5-6	(7-8	9-10)	
To fit chest			
62 - 66	67 - 71	72 - 76	cm
24¹/₂ - 26	26¹/₂ - 28	28¹/₄ - 30	in
Bodice circumference			
86	92	98	cm
34	36¹/₄	38¹/₂	in
Bodice length			
46	50	55	cm
18	19³/₄	21³/₄	in
Sleeve length			
36	39	41	cm
14¹/₄	15¹/₂	16¹/₄	in

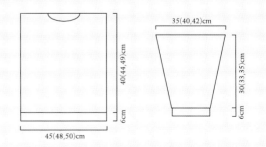

NEEDLES

1 pair 3.75mm needles (USA 5) (UK 9)
1 pair 4.00mm needles (USA 6) (UK 8)
1 pair 4.50mm needles (USA 7) (UK 7)
1 set 3.75mm circular needles (USA 5) (UK 9)

MOSS STITCH

Row 1 (RS) K1, p1 to end.
Row 2 (WS) K the p sts and P the k sts as they face you.
Rows 1 & 2 form Moss stitch pattern.

TENSION

Measured over 10cm (approx. 4").
St st 22.5sts and 30 rows using 4.00mm needles.
Fairisle 23sts and 25rows using 4.50mm needles.

HAWTHORN, VERSION 1
FRONT

Using 3.75mm needles and col A (refer to Graph A for Colour Key), cast on 102(108,114)sts.
Row 1 *P2, k2; rep from* to last p2.
Row 2 *K2, p2; rep from* to last k2.
Rep rows 1 & 2, once.
Change to col B, and cont on rib for 3 more rows, decreasing 1 st in last row [101(107,113)sts].
Now work in Moss st, until band (from beg) measures 6 cm, ending on a WS row. ***Change to 4.00mm needles and work 32(36,42)rows st st. Change to 4.50mm needles.
Next row (RS) Now refer to Bodice Graph A for colour changes and work in fairisle until 58(64,70) graph rows have been worked.
Shape front neck (RS) Patt 42(45,48)sts, turn and leave rem 59(62,65)sts on a holder. Work each side of neck separately.
Keeping patt correct, cast off 2sts at beg (neck edge) of next row, then 2sts on foll alt rows, 3 times [34(37,40)sts] (7 shaping rows).
Work 10 rows straight. Cast off.
Rejoin yarn to rem sts leaving 17sts on a holder at centre. Work second side to match first side, rev all shaping.

BACK

Work back bodice to match front bodice, omitting neck shaping.

SLEEVES

Using 3.75mm needles and col A, (refer to Sleeve Graph B for Colour Key) cast on 42(46,50)sts.
Row 1 *P2, k2; rep from* to last p2.
Row 2 *K2, p2; rep from* to last k2.
Rep rows 1 & 2 once.
Change to col B, and cont on rib for 3 more rows, decreasing 1 st in last row [41(45,49)sts].
Now work in Moss st until 6cm (from beg) have been worked, ending on a WS row.
Change to 4.50mm needles and refer to Sleeve Graph B for colour changes and working in fairisle, work 2 rows.
Shape sleeve Cont in patt, AT THE SAME TIME inc 1st each end next row, then foll 3rd rows 5(8,9)times, then 1st each end foll 4th rows 14(14,14)times [81(91,97)sts] [72(81,84)shaping rows].
Work 0(1,2)rows straight. Cast off.

MAKING UP

Press all pieces gently with a warm iron over a damp cloth. Join shoulder seams. Centre sleeves and join. Join side and sleeve seams.
Neckband With RS facing, using 3.75mm circular needle and col A, pick up and knit 22(24,26)sts down left front, 17sts from holder at centre front, 22(24,26)sts up right front, 29(31,35)sts across back neck [86(94,104)sts]. Work 6 rounds in Moss st, dec 1 st on last round.
Now work 3 rounds k2, p2 rib.
Cast off in rib. Press seams.

HAWTHORN, VERSION 2
FRONT

Using 3.75mm needles and col B (refer to Graph B for Colour Key), cast on 100(104,112)sts.
Work 4 rows k2, p2 rib.
Change to col A and cont in k2, p2 rib until band (from beg) measures 6cm, inc 1(3,1)sts in last WS row [101(107,113)sts].
Change to 4.50mm needles.
Now refer to Graph B for colour changes and patt until 86(96,108)graph rows are completed.
Now work front neck shaping as for Version 1.

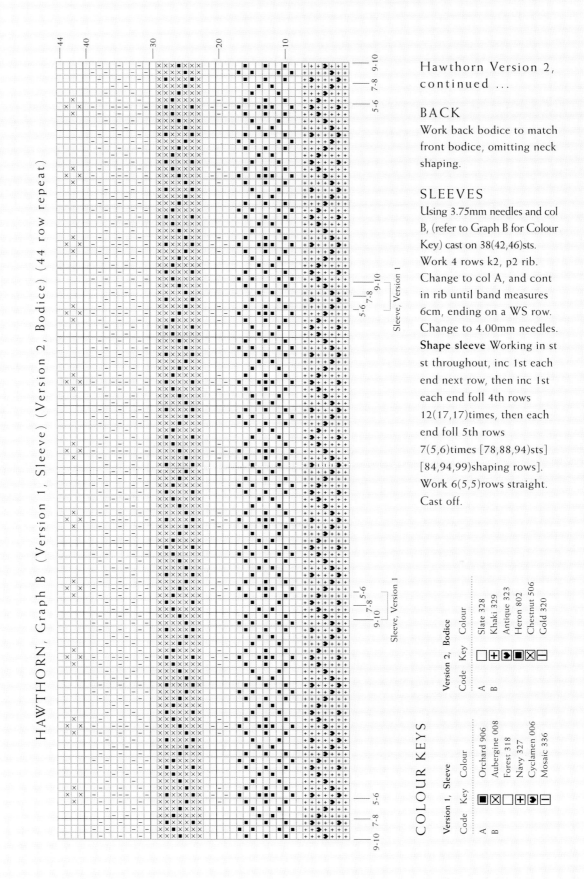

HAWTHORN, Graph B (Version 1, Sleeve) (Version 2, Bodice) (44 row repeat)

Hawthorn Version 2, continued ...

BACK
Work back bodice to match front bodice, omitting neck shaping.

SLEEVES
Using 3.75mm needles and col B, (refer to Graph B for Colour Key) cast on 38(42,46)sts. Work 4 rows k2, p2 rib. Change to col A, and cont in rib until band measures 6cm, ending on a WS row. Change to 4.00mm needles. **Shape sleeve** Working in st st throughout, inc 1st each end next row, then inc 1st each end foll 4th rows 12(17,17)times, then each end foll 5th rows 7(5,6)times [78,88,94)sts] [84,94,99)shaping rows]. Work 6(5,5)rows straight. Cast off.

COLOUR KEYS

Version 1, Sleeve		
Code	Key	Colour
A	■	Orchard 906
	⊠	Aubergine 008
	□	Forest 318
B	+	Navy 327
	◗	Cyclamen 006
	–	Mosaic 336

Version 2, Bodice		
Code	Key	Colour
A	□	Slate 328
B	+	Khaki 329
	◗	Antique 323
	■	Heron 802
	⊠	Chestnut 506
	–	Gold 320

HAWTHORN, Graph A (Versions 1 & 3, Bodice)

COLOUR KEYS

Version 1, Bodice

Code	Key	Colour
A	☒	Forest 318
B	☐	Navy 327
	➕	Cyclamen 005
	·	Aubergine 008
	■	Orchard 906

Version 3, Bodice

Code	Key	Colour
A	☐	Silk 903
B	➕	Owl 801
	☒	Teal 007
	·	Aubergine 008
	■	Heron 802

Hawthorn, Version 2, continued ...

MAKING UP
Work as for Version 1 from * to *.

Neckband With RS facing, using 3.75mm circular needle and col A, pick up and knit 22(24,26)sts down left front, 17sts from holder at centre front, 22(24,26)sts up right front, 29(31,35)sts across back neck [90(96,104)sts]. Work 4cm in rounds of k2, p2 rib. Cast off in rib. Press seams.

HAWTHORN, VERSION 3
FRONT
Using 3.75mm needles and col A (refer to Graph A for Colour Key),cast on 102(108,114)sts.
Row 1 *P2, k2; rep from* to last p2.
Row 2 *K2, p2; rep from* to last k2.
Repeat rows 1 & 2, once.
Cont on rib for 3 more rows, decreasing 1 st in last row [101(107,113)sts].
Now work in Moss st, until band (from beg) measures 6 cm, ending on a WS row.
Now work as for Version 1 from *** to end.

BACK
Using col A and st st throughout (ie: omit colour changes), work back bodice length to match front bodice length, omitting needle size changes and neck shaping.

SLEEVES
Using 3.75mm needles and col A throughout, cast on 38(42,46)sts.
Row 1 *P2, k2; rep from* to last p2.
Row 2 *K2, p2; rep from* to last k2.
Rep rows 1 & 2 once.
Cont on rib for 3 more rows, decreasing 1 st in last row [37(41,45)sts].
Now work in Moss st until 6cm (from beg) have been worked, inc 1 st in last WS row [38(42,46)sts].
Change to 4.00mm needles.
Shape Sleeve Now working in st st, inc 1st at each end next row, then 1st at each end foll 4th rows 12(17,17)times, then on foll 5th rows 7(5,6)times [78(88,94)sts] [84(94,99)shaping rows]. Work 6(5,5)rows straight. Cast off.

MAKING UP
Work as for Version 1.

LAURIE
This unisex lattice cable sweater has drop shoulder shaping. The collar opening is edged with knitted cord, shaped into button loops. A suitable project for the **average skilled knitter** with experience in cable knitting.

Version 1   Version 2

YARN
Jo Sharp 8 ply DK Pure Wool
Hand Knitting Yarn.

Colour	Quantity x 50g balls		
Version 1	5-6	(7-8	9-10)
Pistachio 002	10	12	14
Version 2	5-6	(7-8	9-10)
Chestnut 506	10	12	14

NEEDLES
1 pair 3.75mm needles (USA 5) (UK 9)
1 pair 4.00mm needles (USA 6) (UK 8)
1 pair 3.75mm circular needles (USA 5) (UK 9)
1 pair 3.75mm double pointed needles (USA 5) (UK 9)
1 cable needle

BUTTONS
2 x 1.5cm buttons.

TENSION
Measured over 10cm (approx 4")
using 4.00mm needles
Bodice 28sts and 30rows of Cable Pattern.
Sleeves 23sts and 31rows of Double Moss st.

MEASUREMENTS

(Measurements given in inches are approximate)

Unisex sizing

5-6	(7-8	9-10)	
To fit chest			
62 - 66	67 - 71	72 - 76	cm
24¹/₂ - 26	26¹/₄ - 28	28¹/₄ - 30	in
Bodice circumference			
86	94	102	cm
34	37	40¹/₄	in
Bodice length			
44	48	52	cm
17¹/₄	19	20¹/₂	in
Sleeve length			
30	33	36	cm
11³/₄	13	14¹/₄	in

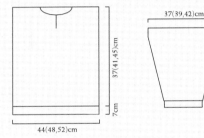

SPECIAL ABBREVIATIONS

C4B (Cable 4 Back) Slip next 2 sts onto a cable needle and leave at back of work, knit next 2 sts from left- hand needle, then knit sts from cable needle.

C3F (Cross 3 Front) Slip next 2 sts onto a cable needle and hold at front of work, knit next st from left-hand needle, then knit sts from cable needle.

T3B (Twist 3 Back) Slip next st onto a cable needle and hold at back of work, knit next 2 sts from left-hand needle, then purl st from cable needle.

T3F (Twist 3 Front) Slip next 2 sts onto a cable needle and hold at front of work, purl next st from left-hand needle, then knit sts from cable needle.

BAND PATTERN

R1 K4,* p2, K4, rep from * to end.

R2 P4,* k2, p4, rep from * to end.

R3 K4,* p2, C4B, p2, k4, rep from * to end.

R4 P4,* k2, p4, rep from * to end.

These 4 rows form pattern repeat.

CABLE PATTERN

Multiple of 12sts + 14.

R1 (RS) P5, k4,* p8, k4; rep from * to last 5 sts, p5.

R2 K5 p4,* k8, p4; rep from * to last 5 sts, k5.

R3 P5, C4B,* p8, C4B; rep from * to last 5 sts, p5.

R4 As 2nd row.

R5 P4, T3B, C3F,* p6, T3B, C3F; rep from * to last 4 sts, p4.

R6 K4, p2, k1, p3,* k6, p2, k1, p3; rep from * to last 4 sts, k4.

R7 P3, T3B, k1, p1, C3F,* p4, T3B, k1, p1, C3F; rep from * to last 3 sts, p3.

R8 K3, p2, k1, p1, k1, p3,* k4, p2, k1, p1, k1, p3; rep from * to last 3 sts, k3.

R9 P2,* T3B,[k1, p1] twice, C3F, p2; rep from * to end.

R10 K2, * p2, k1, [p1, k1] twice, p3, k2; rep from * to end.

R11 P1, * T3B, [k1, p1] 3 times, C3F; rep from * to last st, p1.

R12 K1, p2, k1,[p1,k1] 3 times, * p5, k1, [p1, k1] 3 times; rep from * to last 4 sts, p3, k1.

R13 P1, k3, [p1, k1] 3 times, p1, * C4B, [k1, p1] 4 times; rep from * to last 3 sts, k2, p1.

R14 K1, p3, k1, [p1, k1] 3 times, * p5, k1, [p1, k1] 3 times; rep from * to last 3 sts, p2, k1.

R15 P1, k2, p1, [k1, p1] 3 times, * k5, p1, [k1, p1] 3 times; rep from * to last 4 sts, k3, p1.

R16-18 As rows 12-14.

R19 P1, *T3F, [k1, p1] 3 times, T3B; rep from * to last st, p1.

R20 K2, * p3, k1, [p1, k1] twice, p2, k2, rep from * to end.

R21 P2, *T3F, [k1, p1] twice, T3B, p2; rep from * to end.

R22 K3, p3, k1, p1, k1, p2, * k4, p3, k1, p1, k1, p2; rep from * to last 3 sts, k3.

R23 P3, T3F, k1, p1, T3B, * p4, T3F, k1, p1, T3B; rep from * to last 3 sts, p3.

R24 K4, p3, k1, p2, * k6, p3, k1, p2; rep from * to last 4 sts, k4.

R25 P4, T3F, T3B, * p6, T3F, T3B; rep from * to last 4 sts, p4.

R26-28 Rep 2nd and 3rd rows once, then 2nd row again.

Rep these 28 rows.

Laurie, continued ...

BACK

Using 3.75mm needles, cast on 124(136,148)sts.
Work 24 rows in Band Pattern, dec 1st at each end
of last row [122(134,146)sts].
Change to 4.00mm needles.
Now working in Cable Pattern rep, ** work until
back (incl band) measures 44(48,52)cm. Cast off.

FRONT

Work as for Back to **. Work until front (incl.band)
measures 30(34,38)cm, ending on a WS row.
Make opening (RS) Work 61(67,73)sts, turn and
leave rem 61(67,73)sts on holder.
Work each side of neck separately. Cont working
in patt until front measures 37(41,45)cm, ending
on RS row.
Shape neck (WS) Cast off 3 sts at beg (neck
edge) of next row, then foll alt rows twice, then
dec 1st at neck edge in foll alt rows 5 times
[47(53,59)sts] (15 shaping rows).
Work 6 rows straight. Cast off rem sts.
Rejoin yarn to rem sts and work second side to
match first side, rev all shaping.

SLEEVES

Using 3.75mm needles, cast on 48(48,52)sts.
Work 4cm in Band Pattern, ending on a WS row.
Change to 4.00mm needles.

Now work in Double Moss st as follows;
Row 1 K1, * p1, k1; rep from * to end.
Row 2 P1, * k1, p1; rep from * to end.
Row 3 As row 2.
Row 4 As row 1.
Rep these 4 rows for pattern.
Shape sleeve Keeping patt correct inc 1st at each
end of next row, then on every foll 4th row
18(20,22)times [86(90,98)sts] [73(81,89)shaping
rows]. Work 8(8,10) rows straight.
Cast off in Double Moss st.

MAKING UP

Press all pieces gently with a warm iron over a
damp cloth. Join shoulder seams. Centre sleeves
and join, join side and sleeve seams.
Collar With RS facing, using 3.75mm circular
needle, beginning at centre front, pick-up and knit
26(26,31)sts along right front, 36(36,40)sts across
back neck, 26(26,31)sts along left front,
[88(88,102)sts]. Now work in rows (not rounds) of
k2, p2 rib until collar measures 8cm. Cast off in rib.
Make st st cord Using 3.75mm double pointed
needles, cast on 4 sts. *K4, do not turn work, slide
sts to right end of needle and pull yarn to tighten.
Rep from * for approx 28cm, leave sts on needle,
do not cast off. Position cord along collar opening, making loops for buttons and sew in place.
Sew on buttons. (see illustration in colour pages at
front of book).

MY FAVOURITE SCARF

This simple scarf pattern uses Garter stitch and three colour variations. The boy's scarf is worked in bold
easy stripes while the girl's scarf is decorated with softly contrasting crocheted star or clover motifs.
This project is suitable for a **beginner knitter** with knowledge of **crochet techniques** for the girl's scarves only.

Version 1

Version 2

Version 3

YARN

Jo Sharp 8 ply DK Pure Wool
Hand Knitting Yarn.

Code	Colour	Quantity
Version 1		x 50g balls
A	Cherry 309	1
B	Ebony 902	4
C	Khaki 329	1
Version 2		
A	Silk 903	2
B	Natural 301	2
C	Heron 802	1
Version 3		
A	Winter 904	2
B	Orchard 906	2
C	Heron 802	1

MEASUREMENTS

(Measurements given in inches are approximate)

Length	Width
109cm (43")	22cm (8¾")

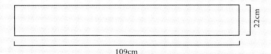

NEEDLES

1 pair 3.25mm needles (USA 3) (UK 10)
1 x 4.00mm crochet hook (USA 6) (UK 8)

TENSION

22 sts & 44 rows measured over 10cm (approx 4")
of Garter stitch, using 3.25mm needles.

VERSION 1

Using 3.25mm needles and col A, cast on 50 sts.
Now working in Garter stitch throughout (knit all
rows) work 4 rows col A, 10 rows col B, 14 rows
col C, 10 rows col B, 36 rows col A, 334 rows col
B, 36 rows col A, 10 rows col B, 14 rows col C, 10
rows col B, work 4 rows col A (482 rows).
Cast off.

VERSION 2

Using 3.25mm needles and col A, cast on 50 sts.
Now working in Garter st throughout (knit all
rows) work 96 rows col A, 290 rows col B, 96 rows
col A (482 rows). Cast off.

MAKING UP

See page 1 for crochet abbreviations
Crochet 6 star motifs as follows;
Using a 4.00mm crochet hook and col C, Ch2
Round 1 5 dc in 2nd ch from hook
Round 2 3 dc in each dc
Round 3 (1 dc in next st, ch6, sl st in 2nd ch
from hook, 1 dc in next ch, 1 htr in next ch, 1 tr
in next ch, 1 dbl tr in next ch, 1 dbl tr in base of
starting dc, sk 2 dc) 4 times, sl st in first dc to join,
fasten off. Sew motifs onto scarf as illustrated in
colour pages at front of book.

VERSION 3

Work scarf as for Version 2.

MAKING UP

Refer to page 1 for crochet abbreviations.
Using a 4.00mm crochet hook and col C, crochet
8 clover motifs as follows;
Ch 5 and join a ring with sl st.
Round 1 14 dc in ring
Round 2 2 dc, 1 leaf [ch 4, (yrh twice, insert
hook in next st, draw up a loop, yrh, draw through
2 loops, yrh, draw through 2 loops) 3 times in
same st. yrh draw through 4 loops, ch 3], 1 dc in
each of next 2 sts, 3 more leaves as above, make
stem [ch 6, work back along these 6 ch with 1 sl st
in each ch], 1 sl st in 1 st dc to close, fasten off.
Sew motifs onto scarf as illustrated in colour pages
at front of book.

ELOISE

This snug cardigan has a decorative rib pattern which fans gently to create a self-shaped shawl collar. This project is suitable for a **beginner to average skilled knitter.**

YARN

Jo Sharp 8 ply DK Pure Wool
Hand Knitting Yarn.

Colour	Quantity x 50g balls		
Version 1	3-4	(5-6	7-8)
Storm 706	7	9	11
Version 2	3-4	(5-6	7-8)
Ink 901	7	9	11

NEEDLES

1 pair 3.25mm needles (USA 3) (UK 10)
1 pair 4.00mm needles (USA 6) (UK 8)
1 pair 3.75mm needles (USA 5) (UK 9)

BUTTONS

5 x 1.5cm buttons.

TENSION

24sts and 28rows measured over 10cm (approx. 4")
of Texture Pattern using 4.00mm needles.

MEASUREMENTS

(Measurements given in inches are approximate)

Sizing

3-4	(5-6	7-8)	
To fit chest			
57 - 61	62 - 66	67 - 71	cm
22¹/₂ - 24	24¹/₂ - 26	26¹/₂ - 28	in
Bodice circumference			
72	82	92	cm
28¹/₂	32¹/₄	36¹/₄	in
Bodice length			
34	38	42	cm
13¹/₂	15	16¹/₂	in
Sleeve length			
30	32	35	cm
11³/₄	12¹/₂	13³/₄	in

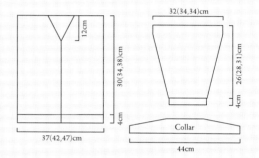

RIB PATTERN

Multiple 4 + 1
Row 1 * (RS) P2, k2; rep from * to last st, p1
Row 2 * (WS) K2, p2; rep from * to last st, k1
Repeat rows 1 and 2.

TEXTURE PATTERN

Multiple 4 + 2
Row 1 (RS) Knit
Row 2 Purl
Row 3 K2 * p2, k2; rep from * to end
Row 4 P2 * k2, p2; rep from * to end
Row 5 Knit
Row 6 Purl
Row 7 As 4th row
Row 8 As 3rd row
These 8 rows form pattern repeat.

BACK

Using 3.25mm needles, cast on 89(101,113)sts.
*Work 4cm in Rib Pattern, inc 1st across last WS
row * [90(102,114)sts].
Change to 4.00mm needles.
Now work in Texture Pattern until back (incl.
band) measures 32(36,40)cm, ending on a WS row.
Shape shoulders (RS) Cast off 11(12,14)sts at beg
next 4 rows, then 11(14,15)sts at beg next 2 rows
[24(26,28)sts] (6 shaping rows). Cast off.

FRONT

Using 3.25mm needles, cast on 45(49,57)sts.
Work as for Back from * to * [46(50,58)sts].
Change to 4.00mm needles.
Cont in patt until front (incl. band) measures
22(26,30)cm, ending on a WS row.
Shape neck (RS) Dec 2(0,2)sts at beg (neck edge)
on next row, then 1 st on foll alt rows, 11(12,13)times
[33(38,43)sts] [23(25,27)shaping rows].
Work 7(5,3) rows straight.
Shape shoulder (RS) Cast off 11(12,14)sts at beg
next and foll alt row, then cast off rem 11(14,15)sts.
Work second side to match first side, rev all shaping.

SLEEVES

Using 3.25mm needles, cast on 37(41,41)sts.
Work as for Back from * to * [38(42,42)sts].
Change to 4.00mm needles.

Shape sleeve Now working in Texture Pattern,
inc 1st at each end every 3rd row 11(10,4) times,
then every 4th row 8(10,16)times [76(82,82)sts]
[65(70,76) shaping rows].
Work 9(10,10)rows straight. Cast off.

MAKING UP

Press all pieces gently on WS, using a warm iron
over a damp cloth. Using Backstitch, join shoulder
seams. Centre sleeves and join, join side and
sleeve seams.
Button Band With RS facing, using 3.75mm needles, pick up and knit 65(69,73)sts along left
front. Work 7 rows in rib pattern beg with a WS
row. Cast off in rib. Mark position on band for 5
buttons, the first to come 2cm from lower edge,
the last to come 2cm from top of band, the other
3 spaced evenly between.
Buttonhole Band Work as for button band,
making 5 corresponding buttonholes (buttonhole
instructions on page 2).
Collar Using 3.75mm needles, cast on 121sts.
Work 10 rows in rib patt.
Shape collar Cast off 3 sts at beg of next 4 rows,
then 4 sts at beg next 6 rows, then 5 sts at beg
next 10 rows (35sts) (30 rows). Cast off in rib.
Attach collar to neck opening, joining to button
bands at front. Sew buttons in position.
Press seams.

TRULY TIMELESS

This unisex sweater is comfortable & snug with a zip up collar that provides extra warmth.
Suitable for a **beginner / average skilled knitter.**

Sweaters
Version 1 (boy), Version 2 (girl)

YARN
Jo Sharp 8 ply DK Pure Wool Hand Knitting Yarn .

Colour	Quantity x 50g balls		
Version 1	5-6	(7-8	9-10)
Monsoon 704	9	10	11
Version 2	5-6	(7-8	9-10)
Haze 701	9	10	11

NEEDLES & ZIP
1 pair 3.75mm needles (USA 5) (UK 9),
1 pair 4.00mm needles (USA 6) (UK 8)
1 set 4.00mm circular needles (USA 6) (UK 8)
1 x 18cm zip (7")

See next page for Size Diagram & Measurements.

Truly Timeless, continued....

MEASUREMENTS

(Measurements given in inches are approximate)

Unisex Sizing

5-6	(7-8	9-10)	
To fit chest			
62 - 66	67 - 71	72 - 76	cm
24¹/₂ - 26	26¹/₂ - 28	28¹/₂ - 30	in
Bodice circumference			
86	94	102	cm
34	37	40¹/₄	in
Bodice length			
45	49	53	cm
17³/₄	19¹/₄	21	in
Sleeve length			
34	37	40	cm
13¹/₂	14¹/₂	15³/₄	in

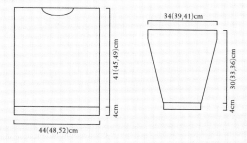

TENSION

22.5sts and 30 rows measured over 10cm
(approx. 4") Rib Pattern using 4.00mm needles.

RIB PATTERN

Multiple 10 + 9

Row 1 Knit.

Row 2 P9 * Kb1, p9 rep from * to end.

These 2 rows form pattern repeat.

BACK

Using 3.75mm needles, cast on 99(108,117)sts and
work 4cm in k2, p1 rib, increasing 0(1,2)sts across
last WS row [99(109,119)sts].

Change to 4.00mm needles. * Patt until back (incl.
band) measures 43(47,51)cm, ending on a WS row.

Shape back neck (RS) Work 49(54,59)sts, turn,
leave rem 50(55,60)sts on a holder.

Cast off 5(6,5)sts at beg next row, then 4(4,5)sts
on foll alt rows twice. Work 1 row. Cast off rem
36(40,44)sts. With RS facing, rejoin yarn to rem
sts. Cast off 6(7,6)sts at beg next row, then
4(4,5)sts at neck edge on foll alt rows twice.
Work 1 row. Cast off rem 36(40,44)sts.

FRONT

Work as for back to *. Patt until front (incl. band)
measures 29(31,35)cm, ending on a WS row.

Make zip opening (RS) Work 49(54,59)sts, turn,
leave rem 50(55,60)sts on a holder. Patt a further
12cm, ending on a RS row.

Shape front neck (WS) Cast off 5(6,7)sts at beg
(neck edge) of next row **, then 2sts on next row,
then on foll alt rows 3 times [36(40,44)sts]
(8 shaping rows). Work 11 rows without shaping.
Cast off. Rejoin yarn to rem sts. Cast off 6(7,8)sts
at beg next row and work as for left side from **.

SLEEVES

Using 3.75mm needles, cast on 28(32,36)sts.
Work 4cm in K2, p1 rib, inc 10sts evenly across
last WS row [38(42,46)sts].
Change to 4.00mm needles.

Shape sleeve Now work in Rib Pattern as for
back and front AT THE SAME TIME inc 1st each
end next row, then foll 4th rows, 12(17,17)times,
then foll 5th rows 7(5,6)times [78(88,94)sts]
[84(94,99)rows].
Work 7(6,10)rows straight. Cast off.

MAKING UP

Press all pieces gently on WS with a warm iron
over a damp cloth. Using Backstitch, join shoulder
seams. Centre sleeves and join. Join side and
sleeve seams.

Note: Collar is worked with a circular needle in
rows, not rounds.

Collar With RS facing, using 4.00mm circular
needle, pick up and k31(33,33)sts along right
front neck, 36 sts across back neck, 31(33,33)sts
along left front neck [98(102,102)sts].
Work 12cm K2, p2 rib. Cast off evenly in rib.
Sew zip into place. Fold collar to inside of neck,
stitch into place. Press seams.

HARPER

A comfortable, textured drop shoulder sweater in four colour variations. This easy slip stitch pattern creates a soft, gently ribbed fabric. This project is suitable for the **beginner knitter**.

Version 1

Version 2

Version 3

Version 4

YARN
Jo Sharp 8 ply DK Pure Wool
Hand Knitting Yarn.

Code	Colour	Quantity x 50g balls		
Version 1		5-6	(7-8	9-10)
A	Owl 801	9	9	10

Code	Colour			
Version 2		5-6	(7-8	9-10)
A	Khaki 329	3	4	4
B	Heron 802	4	5	5
C	Ink 901	2	2	2

Code	Colour			
Version 3		5-6	(7-8	9-10)
A	Ginger 322	3	4	4
B	Teal 007	3	4	4
C	Brick 333	1	1	1
D	Gold 320	1	1	1
E	Khaki 329	1	2	2

Code	Colour			
Version 4		5-6	(7-8	9-10)
A	Ebony 902	3	4	4
B	Hull 705	3	4	4
C	Owl 801	1	1	1
D	Ivory 703	1	1	1
E	Camel 005	1	2	2

MEASUREMENTS
(Measurements given in inches are approximate)

Sizing

5-6	(7-8	9-10)	
To fit chest			
62 - 66	67 - 71	72 - 76	cm
24½ - 26	26½ - 28	28½ - 30	in
Bodice circumference			
84	89	94	cm
33	35	37	in
Bodice length			
44	48	52	cm
17¼	19	20½	in
Sleeve length			
33	36	39	cm
13	14¼	15½	in

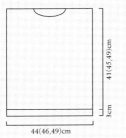

41(45,49)cm

3cm

44(46,49)cm

40(42,44)cm

31(34,37)cm

2cm

Harper, continued...

NEEDLES

1 pair 3.75mm needles (USA 5) (UK 9)
1 pair 4.50mm needles (USA 7) (UK 7)

TENSION

21.5sts and 34 rows measured over 10cm
(approx. 4") Texture Pattern using 4.50mm
needles.

TEXTURE PATTERN

Multiple 4+2
Row 1 (RS) K2,* p2, k2; rep from * to end.
Row 2 P2,* keeping yarn at front of work sl 2
purlwise, p2; rep from * to end.
Rep these 2 rows.

FRONT

(Note: use col A throughout for Version 1)
Using 3.75mm needles and col A, cast on
94(98,106)sts.
Work 3cm in Texture Pattern, ending on a WS
row. Change to 4.50mm needles, patt until work
(from beg) measures 20(22,25)cm, ending on a
WS row.
Change to col C (version 2) col E (version 3 & 4),
patt 4cm, ending on a WS row. Change to col B,
patt until work (from beg) measures 38(42,46)cm,
ending on a WS row.
Shape neck (RS) Patt 39(41,45)sts, turn, leave
rem sts on a holder. Cast off 2 sts at beg (neck
edge) of next row, then 2 sts on foll alt rows, 3
times [31(33,37)sts] (7 shaping rows).
Work 13 rows straight. Cast off.
With RS facing, rejoin yarn to rem sts. Leave 16sts
on holder. Work second side to match first side,
rev all shaping.

BACK

Work as for front, omitting neck shaping.

SLEEVES

(**Version 1 & 2**) (Version 1; use col A throughout)
Using 3.75mm needles and col B, cast on 38(42,46)sts.

Work 3cm in Texture Patt, ending on a WS row.
Change to 4.50mm needles.
Shape sleeve Cont in patt making colour changes
as follows; work 66(76,86)rows in col B, 34 rows
in col C, 6 rows in col A, AT THE SAME TIME,
inc 1 st each end of every 4th row, 20(10,0)times,
then every 5th row, 4(14,24)times [86(90,94)sts]
[100(110,120)shaping rows].
Work 6 rows straight. Cast off.

SLEEVES

(**Version 3 & 4**)
Using 3.75mm needles and col A, cast on
38(42,46)sts. Patt 4 rows, change to col B, patt 4
rows. Change to 4.50mm needles.
Shape sleeve Cont in patt, making colour
changes as follows; **Rows 1-4** col B, **Rows 5-8**
col C, **Rows 9 & 10** col D, **Rows 11 & 12** col E,
Row 13 col B, **Rows 14-16** col E,
Rows 17 & 18 col A. Repeat rows 1-18 throughout sleeve AT THE SAME TIME inc 1st each end
of every 4th row, 20(10,0)times, then every 5th
row, 4(14,24)times [86(90,94)sts]
[100(110,120)shaping rows].
Work 6 rows straight. Cast off

MAKING UP

Note: Use col A throughout for Version 1.
Press all pieces gently on WS with a warm iron
over a damp cloth. Using Backstitch, join right
shoulder seam.
Neckband With RS facing, using 3.75mm needles
and col C, pick up and knit 22 sts along left front,
16 sts from holder at centre, 22 sts along right
front, 32 sts across back neck (92 sts).
Work 3 rows in Garter st (knit all rows).
Next row (RS) Work 4 rows in Texture Pattern.
Change to col B, patt 8 rows. Cast off in rib.
Centre sleeves and join, join side and sleeve
seams. Press seams

TILLY DOLL

This doll is a very easy project, suitable for a **beginner knitter**.

Version 1 (right) & Version 2 (left)

YARN

Jo Sharp 8 ply DK Pure Wool
Hand Knitting Yarn.

Code	Colour	Quantity	
Version 1		50g balls	Metres
A	Brick 333	1	(or 28 metres)
B	Tangerine 003	1	(or 10 metres)
C	Renaissance 312	1	(or 23 metres)
D	Pistachio 002	1	(or 9 metres)
E	Antique 323	1	(or 7 metres)

Code	Colour	Quantity	
Version 2			
A	Embers 804	1	(or 28 metres)
B	Pistachio 002	1	(or 10 metres)
C	Cyclamen 006	1	(or 23 metres)
D	Citrus 509	1	(or 9 metres)
E	Ebony 902	1	(or 7 metres)

MEASUREMENTS

Doll Height 31cm (approx 12¼")

NEEDLES

1 pair 3.25mm needles (USA 3) (UK 10)

TENSION

24sts and 32rows measured over 10cm (approx. 4")
st st using 3.25mm needles.

STUFFING

For this doll, use natural wool fibre stuffing rather than synthetic stuffing to give the doll weight. This makes the doll more satisfying to play with.

VERSION 1

** **Legs (make 2)** Using 3.25mm needles and col A, cast on 7 sts. **Row 1** Knit.
Row 2 Purl. **Row 3** K1, m1, k to the last 2 sts, m1, k3 (9sts). **Row 4** Purl. **Row 5** K1, m1, k to the last 2 st, m1, k3 (11sts). **Row 6** Purl.
Row 7 K1, m1, k to the last 2 st, m1, k3 (13sts).
Row 8 Purl. **Row 9** K1, m1, k to the last 2 st, m1, k3 (15sts). **Row 10 (WS)** Knit.
Row 11 (RS) Knit. **Row 12 (WS)** Knit.
Next row (RS) Now working in st st, work *2 rows col B, 2 rows col A; rep from * 9 times (40 rows st st stripes). Leave sts on holder. Thread two legs onto left needle. Now using col A, pick up and knit 30 sts across top of both legs.
Cont in st st for a further 9 rows.
Bodice (RS) Using col C work 7 rows in Garter st (knit all rows).**
Next row (WS) Purl.
Next row (RS) Knit.
Next row (WS) P1 col C, p1 col D *p2 col C, p2 col D; rep from * to last 2 sts, p1 col D, p1 col C. Work 2 rows st st using col C.
Next row (RS) K1 col C, k1 col D *k2 col C, k2 col D; rep from * to last 2 sts, k1 col D, k1 col C. Work 4 rows st st using col C. *** (WS) Work 4 rows Garter st (k all rows). Cast off.
Hands & Arms (make 2)
Hand Using 3.25mm needles and col E, cast on 6 sts. Work 2 rows st st.
Shape hand Inc 1 st at each end of next row, then foll alt row (10sts).
Work 4 rows straight (9 rows).
Cuff (WS) Using col C, purl.
Next row Purl. **Next row** Knit.
Arm (RS) Col D, knit.
Next row (WS) Col D, Purl.
Now working in st st, work * 1 row col C, 1 row col D; repeat from * 7 times (18 striped st st rows in all). Change to col C and cont in st st for a further 10 rows. Cast off.***

Tilly Doll, continued...

MAKING UP

Fold legs and body in half lengthwise and sew along leg seams and up centre back, leaving an opening at crotch for stuffing. Stuff legs and close opening.

Make front neck & head Using col C, and working in st st throughout, pick up and knit 10 sts at centre at top of front bodice, work 1 row.
Change to col E.

Shape head Dec 1 st at each end of next 2 rows. Work 1 row (6 sts). Inc 1 st at each end of next 2 rows (10sts). Work 9 rows straight. Cast off 1 st at each end of next 3 rows. Cast off rem 4 sts.

Make back head Now using col C, and working in st st throughout, pick up and knit 10 sts at centre at top of back bodice, work 1 row.
Change to col A and shape back of head to match front of head.

Complete Making Up Now finish stuffing body and sew along top bodice, closing neck as well. Embroider eyes using col C, and mouth using col A. Sew head seams together, leaving an opening for stuffing. Stuff head and close opening.

Make hair Using col A, thread a strand of yarn through top of head and tie in a knot at base to secure, leaving 2, 4cm ends. Continue making hair along top of head until desired amount is attached. Now using a darning needle, split the yarn to fray hair.

Attach arms Fold arms in half lengthwise and sew along seam, then stuff and join to body just below shoulder as illustrated.

VERSION 2

Make as for Version 1 from ** to **.
Work 10 rows st st using col C.
Continue as for Version 1 from *** to ***.

MAKING UP

Make up as for Version 1, adding Lazy Daisy flowers to front bodice, using col D for petals & col E for French Knots at centres of flowers. Divide hair into even bunches, then tie & sew bows using col D. Use col B for eyes and col C for mouth.

SIENNE

This simple to knit hooded jacket is worked with two contrasting strands of yarn together to create extra warmth. Two different effects are achieved by sewing the garment together with either the right side or wrong side facing.
Knitted in Stocking stitch, this project is ideal for a **beginner knitter**.

Version 1   Version 2

YARN
Jo Sharp 8 ply DK Pure Wool
Hand Knitting Yarn.

Code	Colour	Quantity x 50g balls		
Version 1		5-6	7-8	9-10
A	Hull 705	7	8	9
B	Monsoon 704	7	8	9
Version 2		5-6	7-8	9-10
A	Ink 901	7	8	9
B	Storm 706	7	8	9

NEEDLES
1 pair 6.00mm (USA 10) (UK 4)
1 pair 6.50mm (USA 10.5) (UK 3)

BUTTONS
5 x 2.5mm buttons.

TENSION
14.5 sts and 19 rows measured over 10cm (approx. 4") of st st, using 6.50mm needles and working with 2 strands (cols A & B) of yarn together.

MEASUREMENTS

(Measurements given in inches are approximate)

Unisex sizing

5-6	(7-8	9-10)	
To fit chest			
62 - 66	67 - 71	72 - 76	cm
24¹/₂ - 26	26¹/₄ - 28	28¹/₄ - 30	in
Bodice circumference			
79	89	101	cm
31	35	39³/₄	in
Bodice Length			
49	53	57	cm
19¹/₄	21	22¹/₂	in
Sleeve Length			
36.5	39	41	cm
14¹/₄	15¹/₄	16¹/₄	in

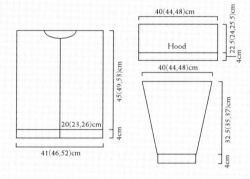

PATTERN

Note: Use cols A & B knitted together throughout.

LEFT FRONT

Using 6.00mm needles, cast on 30(34,38)sts.
Work 6 rows k1, p1 rib.
Change to 6.50mm needles and beg with a K row, work in st st until work (incl. band) measures 44(48,52)cm, ending on a (knit row, version 1) or (purl row, version 2).
Shape front neck Cast off 6 sts at beg (neck edge) of next row, then 1 st on foll alt rows, 5 times [19(23,27)sts].
Work 3 rows. Cast off.

RIGHT FRONT

Work as for Left Front, rev all shaping.

BACK

Using 6.00mm needles cast on 60(68,76)sts.
Work 6 rows k1, p1 rib. Change to 6.50mm needles and beg with a K row, work in st st until back bodice matches front bodice length.
Cast off.

SLEEVES

Using 6.00mm needles, cast on 30(34,40)sts.
Work 6 rows k1, p1 rib.
Change to 6.50mm needles.
Shape sleeve Working in st st, inc 1st at each end of every 4th row 14(15,15)times [58(64,70)sts] [56(60,60)shaping rows]. Work 5(5,9)rows straight. Cast off.

Sienne, cont ...

HOOD

Using 6.00mm needles, cast on 74(78,82)sts.
Work 6 rows k1, p1 rib. Change to 6.50mm
needles and beg with a K row, work in st st until
work measures 26.5(28,29.5)cm. Cast off.

MAKING UP

Note: Version 1 uses WS of fabric on outside of
garment, Version 2 uses RS of fabric on outside of
garment. Press all pieces, except ribbing, gently
on WS (or RS if using WS on outside) using a
warm iron over a damp cloth. Using Edge to Edge
stitch throughout, join shoulder seams. Centre
sleeves and join. Join side and sleeve seams. Fold
hood in half and join along cast off edge. Centre
seam of hood to centre back and sew into place.
Button band Using 6.00mm needles, with RS facing, pick up and k 53(57, 63)sts along left front
for a girl's jacket or right front for a boy's jacket.
Work 5 rows k1 p1 rib. Cast off loosely.
Mark positions for 5 buttons, the first to come
2cm from bottom edge, the last to come 2cm from
top of band, the rem 3 to be spaced evenly
between.
Buttonhole band Using 6.00mm needles, with RS
facing, pick up 53(57,63)sts along right front for a
girl's jacket or left front for a boy's jacket.
Work 1 row k1 p1 rib.
Next 2 rows Buttonhole rows (see page 2 for
instructions)
Work a further 2 rows rib. Cast off.

LIZA

A drop shoulder cardigan with Moss stitch collar
and bands. This project is suitable for a knitter
with experience in **Intarsia (picture) knitting.**

Version 1   Version 2

YARN

Jo Sharp 8 ply DK Pure Wool
Hand Knitting Yarn.

Colour	Quantity x 50g balls		
Version 1	3-4	(5-6	7-8)
Navy 327	4	4	5
Eucalypt 502	2	2	2
Teal 007	1	1	1
Antique 323	1	2	2
Ginger 322	1	1	2
Plum 505	1	1	2
Terracotta 332	1	1	1
Summer 001	1	1	1
Mosaic 336	1	1	1
Version 2	3-4	(5-6	7-8)
Silk 903	4	4	5
Teal 007	2	2	2
Camel 005	1	1	1
Owl 801	1	2	2
Natural 301	1	1	2
Aubergine 008	1	1	2
Heron 802	1	1	1
Summer 001	1	1	1
Cyclamen 006	1	1	1

MEASUREMENTS

(Measurements given in inches are approximate)

Sizing

3-4	(5-6	7-8)	
To fit chest			
57 - 61	62 - 66	67 - 71	cm
22¹/₂ - 24	24¹/₂ - 26	26¹/₂ - 28	in
Bodice circumference			
74	82	92	cm
29¹/₄	32¹/₄	36¹/₄	in
Bodice length			
45	47	50	cm
17³/₄	18¹/₂	19¹/₂	in
Sleeve length (with cuff folded back)			
31	34	37	cm
12¹/₄	13¹/₂	14¹/₂	in

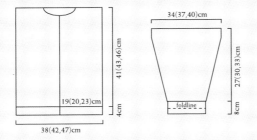

NEEDLES

1 pair 3.75mm needles (USA 5) (UK 9)

1 pair 4.00mm needles (USA 6) (UK 8)

BUTTONS

Size 3-4   5 x 1.5cm buttons.

Sizes 5-6 & 7-8   6 x 1.5cm buttons.

TENSION

22.5sts and 30 rows measured over 10cm

(approx. 4") st st & Intarsia using 4.00mm needles.

MOSS STITCH

Row 1 (RS) K1, p1 to end.

Row 2 (WS) K the p sts and P the k sts as they face you.

Rows 1 & 2 form Moss stitch pattern.

BACK

Using 3.75mm needles and col A, cast on 86(94,106)sts. * Work 12 rows in Moss st. Change to 4.00mm needles.

Now working in st st, refer to graph for pattern placement and colour changes **.

Work 120(126,134)rows.

Shape shoulders (RS) Keeping patt correct, cast off 10(12,14)sts at beg next 4 rows.

Cast off rem 46(46,50)sts.

LEFT FRONT

Using 3.75mm needles and col A, cast on 42(46,52)sts.

Work as for Back from * to **.

Work 107(113,121) rows.

Shape neck (WS) Cast off 2sts at beg (neck edge) of next row, then 2 sts on foll alt rows twice, then 1 st on foll alt row once, then 1 st on every row, 4 times. [31(35,41)sts] [11 shaping rows].

Work 2 rows straight.

Shape shoulder (RS) Cast off 10(12,14)sts at beg of next row then on foll alt row once.

Work 1 row. Cast off rem 11(11,13)sts.

RIGHT FRONT

Work as for left front, reverse all shaping.

SLEEVES

Using 3.75mm needles and col A, cast on 34(38,42)sts. Work 24 rows in Moss st.

Shape sleeve (RS) Now working in st st and referring to graph for pattern placement and colour changes, AT THE SAME TIME inc 1 st at each end of every 3rd row, 10(10,8)times, then every 4th row 11(13,16)times [76(84,90)sts] [74(82,88)shaping rows].

Work 6(8,10) rows straight. Cast off.

MAKING UP

Press all pieces gently with a warm iron over a damp cloth. Join shoulder seams. Centre sleeves and join, join side sleeve seams, using Edge to Edge stitch on bands.

Button Band Using 3.75mm needles and col A, cast on 7sts. Work in Moss st until band (when slightly stretched) is the same length as the front, to beg of neck shaping.

LIZA, Bodice Graph

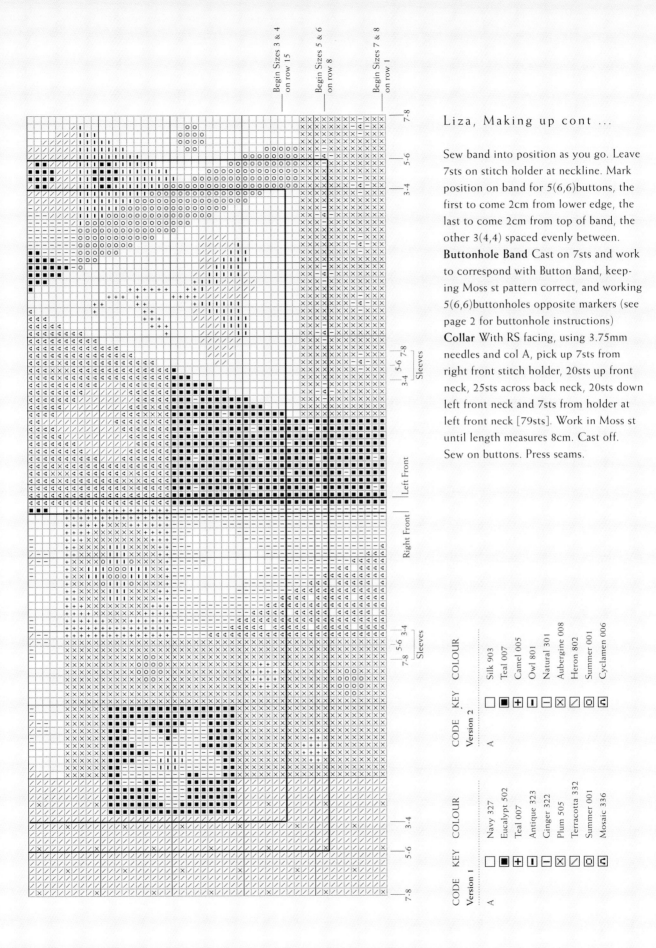

Begin Sizes 3 & 4
on row 15

Begin Sizes 5 & 6
on row 8

Begin Sizes 7 & 8
on row 1

7-8
5-6
3-4

5-6 7-8
3-4 Sleeves

Left Front
Right Front

7-8 3-4
5-6 Sleeves

3-4
5-6
7-8

Liza, Making up cont ...

Sew band into position as you go. Leave 7sts on stitch holder at neckline. Mark position on band for 5(6,6)buttons, the first to come 2cm from lower edge, the last to come 2cm from top of band, the other 3(4,4) spaced evenly between.

Buttonhole Band Cast on 7sts and work to correspond with Button Band, keeping Moss st pattern correct, and working 5(6,6)buttonholes opposite markers (see page 2 for buttonhole instructions)

Collar With RS facing, using 3.75mm needles and col A, pick up 7sts from right front stitch holder, 20sts up front neck, 25sts across back neck, 20sts down left front neck and 7sts from holder at left front neck [79sts]. Work in Moss st until length measures 8cm. Cast off. Sew on buttons. Press seams.

CODE	KEY	COLOUR		
Version 2				
A		Silk 903		
	■	Teal 007		
	✚	Camel 005		
	I	Owl 801		
	−	Natural 301		
	✕	Aubergine 008		
	╱	Heron 802		
	▢	Summer 001		
	⊏	Cyclamen 006		

CODE	KEY	COLOUR		
Version 1				
A		Navy 327		
	■	Eucalypt 502		
	✚	Teal 007		
	I	Antique 323		
	−	Ginger 322		
	✕	Plum 505		
	╱	Terracotta 332		
	▢	Summer 001		
	⊏	Mosaic 336		

27

ANNABEL

This skirt is slightly shaped at the base and is completed with elastic at the waist. The daisy version requires **Intarsia experience** and the striped version is suitable for a **beginner knitter**.

Version 1   Version 2

MEASUREMENTS

(Measurements given in inches are approximate)

Sizing

3-4	(5-6	7-8)

Circumference (before gathering with elastic)

76	80	86	cm
30	31½	34	in

Skirt length

30	32.5	36	cm
11¼	12¾	14¼	in

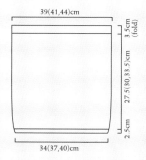

39(41,44)cm

3.5cm (fold)

27.5(30,33.5)cm

2.5cm

34(37,40)cm

NEEDLES

1 pair 3.25mm needles (USA 3) (UK 10)

1 pair 4.00mm needles (USA 6) (UK 8)

YARN

Jo Sharp 8 ply DK Pure Wool
Hand Knitting Yarn.

Code	Key	Colour	Quantity x 50g balls		
Version 1			3-4	(5-6	7-8)
A	☐	Mulberry 325	3	4	4
	☒	Jade 316	1	1	1
	⊟	Lilac 324	1	1	1
	■	Mosaic 336	1	1	1

Version 2			3-4	(5-6	7-8)
A		Renaissance 312	2	2	2
B		Cyclamen 006	1	1	2
C		Amethyst 503	1	1	1
D		Chartreuse 330	1	1	1
E		Brick 333	1	1	1
F		Jade 316	1	1	1

COLOUR SEQUENCE

Rows 1-2 col B, **Row 3** col C, **Row 4** col B,
Row 5 col D, **Row 6** col A, **Row 7** col E,
Row 8 col F, **Rows 9-11** col A.
Repeat these 11 rows throughout.

TENSION

22.5 sts and 30 rows measured over 10cm
(approx 4″) st st, or st st and Intarsia, using
4.00mm needles.

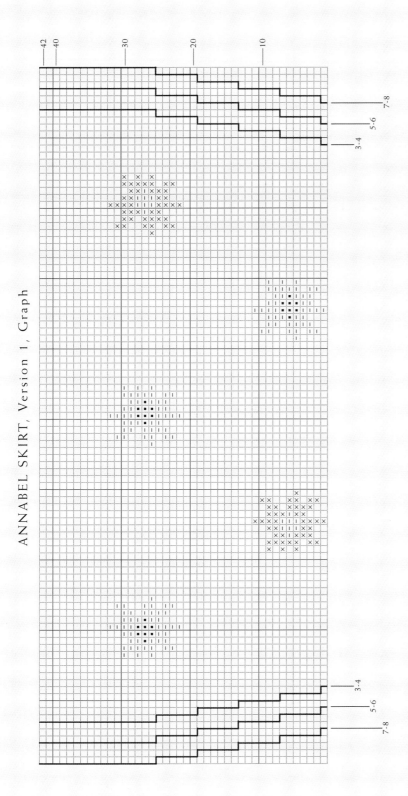

ANNABEL SKIRT, Version 1, Graph

VERSION 1
CODE KEY COLOUR

A

	Mulberry 325
☒	Jade 316
Ɪ	Lilac 324
■	Mosaic 336

MOSS STITCH
Row 1 (RS) K1, p1 to end.
Row 2 (WS) K the p sts and P the k sts
as they face you.
Rows 1 & 2 form Moss stitch pattern.

FRONT
Using 3.25mm needles and col A, cast on
77(83,89)sts. Work 2.5cm in Moss st.
Change to 4.00mm needles.
Now working in st st, (**Version 1** refer to
graph for pattern repeat, placement and
colour changes), (**Version 2** refer to
colour sequence, beg with Row 1)
Work 1 row.
Shape sides Keeping patt correct, inc 1
st at each end of next row, then foll 6th
rows, 4 times [87(93,99)sts] (25 shaping
rows).
Cont working in repeat without shaping
until 82(90,100) patt rows have been
worked.
Make foldline Next row (RS) Purl.
Next row (WS) Purl.
Next row (RS) Knit.
Work a further 8 rows st st. Cast off.

BACK
Make back piece to match front piece.

MAKING UP
Press pieces gently on WS using a warm
iron over a damp cloth. Using
Backstitch, join side seams. Fold waist-
band to inside and slip stitch into place.
Insert elastic. Press seams.

AMELIA

This tunic is loose fitting, drop shouldered and shown in two variations. Both versions require **Intarsia experience** although versions two and three are suitable for a **beginner Intarsia knitter.**
The tunic features Moss stitch borders, side slits at the base and a Moss stitch collar with crochet edging.

Version 1

Version 2

Version 3

NEEDLES

1 pair 4.00mm needles (USA 6) (UK 8)
3.25mm circular needle (USA 10) (UK 3)
3.00mm crochet hook   (USA 3⁴) (UK 11)

YARN

Jo Sharp 8 ply DK Pure Wool
Hand Knitting Yarn.

Code	Colour	Quantity x 50g balls		
Version 1		3-4	(5-6	7-8)
A	Amethyst 503	6	7	7
	Antique 323	1	1	1
	Wine 307	1	1	1
	Ruby 326	1	1	1
	Gold 320	1	1	1
	Violet 319	1	1	1
	Cape 508	1	1	1
	Olive 313	1	1	1
	Forest 318	1	1	1
Version 2		3-4	(5-6	7-8)
A	Cyclamen 006	7	8	8
	Chartreuse 330	1	1	1
	Amethyst 503	1	1	1
Version 3		3-4	(5-6	7-8)
A	Mosaic 336	7	8	8
	Cyclamen 006	1	1	1
	Citrus 509	1	1	1

MEASUREMENTS

(Measurements given in inches are approximate)

Sizes			
3-4	(5-6	7-8)	
To fit chest			
57 - 61	62 - 66	67 - 71	cm
22¹/₂ - 24	24¹/₂ - 26	26¹/₂ - 28	in
Bodice circumference			
76	82	92	cm
30	32¹/₄	36¹/₄	ins
Bodice length			
47	50	52	cm
18¹/₂	19³/₄	20¹/₂	ins
Sleeve length			
31	34	37	cm
12¹/₄	13¹/₂	14¹/₂	ins

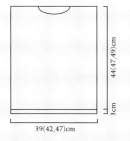

34(38,40)cm

44(47,49)cm

3cm

28(31,34)cm

3cm

39(42,47)cm

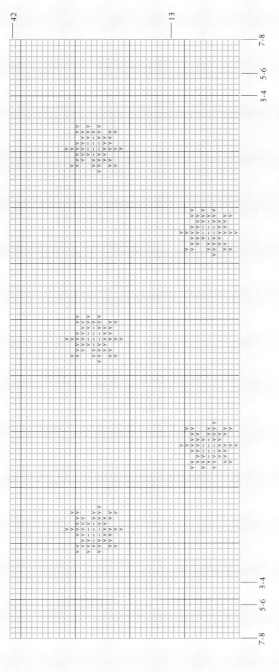

AMELIA Versions 2 & 3, Bodice (Graph B)

KEY COLOUR
Version 2

☐ Cyclamen 006
Ⓥ Chartreuse 330
Ⅰ Amethyst 503

Version 3

☐ Mosaic 336
Ⓥ Cyclamen 006
Ⅰ Citrus 509

TENSION
22.5sts and 30 rows measured over 10cm (approx. 4")
st st & Intarsia, using 4.00mm needles.

MOSS STITCH
Row 1 (RS) K1, p1.
Row 2 (WS) Knit the purl sts and purl the knit sts, as they face you.
Rows 1 & 2 form pattern.

AMELIA, Version 1
FRONT
*Using 4.00mm needles and col A, cast on 87(95,107)sts. Work 10
rows in Moss st.
Moss edge for side opening, Row 1 (RS) Work 5sts Moss st, knit
to last 5sts, Moss st to end.
Moss edge for side opening, Row 2 (WS) Work 5sts Moss st, purl
to last 5sts, Moss st to end.
Rpt Moss st edging rows 1 & 2, 4 times [20 rows from beg]. *
Now refer to Amelia Graph A for colour changes and working in st
st & intarsia, complete 97 graph rows. Now using col A, work
11(17,23)rows [128(134,140)rows from beg].
**Shape neck (RS) Work 38(42,48)sts, turn and leave rem
49(53,59)sts on a holder. Cast off 2 sts at beg (neck edge) on next
row, then foll alt rows twice, then 1 st on next row, then every foll
row, 4 times. Work 1 row [27(31,37)sts] [139(145,151)rows].
Shape shoulders (RS) Cast off 9(10,12)sts at beg of next and foll
alt row. Work 1 row. Cast off rem 9(11,13)sts. Rejoin yarn to rem
sts, leaving 11 sts on holder at centre. Work second side to match
first side, rev all shaping.

BACK
Using 4.00mm needles and col A throughout, work back bodice to
match front bodice, omitting neck shaping and incorporating shoulder shaping into last 4 rows as follows; cast off 9(10,12)sts at beg of
next RS row, then every foll row, 3 times. Cast off rem 51(55,59)sts.

SLEEVES
Using 4.00mm needles & col A, cast on 40(48,48)sts.
Work 10 rows in Moss st.
Shape sleeve Now refer to Amelia Sleeve Graph for colour changes
and working in st st, AT THE SAME TIME inc 1 st at each end of
every 4th row, 12 times, then every 5th row 6(7,9)times
[76(86,90)sts] [78(83,93)graph rows].
Work 6(9,9)rows straight. Cast off loosely and evenly.

MAKING UP
Press all pieces gently on WS using a warm iron over a damp cloth.
Using Backstitch, join shoulder seams. Centre sleeves and join. Join
sleeve seams. Join side seams, leaving Moss st edges open to form
side slits.

AMELIA Version 1, Bodice (Graph A)

Code	Key	Colour
A	☐	Amethyst 503
	V	Antique 323
	+	Wine 307
	◻	Ruby 326
	I	Gold 320
	−	Violet 319
	◣	Cape 508
	╱	Olive 313
	·	Forest 318

Amelia (Version 1), Making Up, continued...
Collar With RS facing, using a 3.25mm circular needle and col A, pick up and K 20 sts down left side front neck, 11 sts from st holder at centre front, 20 sts up right side front neck, 33 sts across back neck [84 sts]. Work 16 rounds in Moss st. Cast off. Using a 3.00mm crochet hook (refer to page 1 for crochet abbreviations), work 1 row dc along cast off edge of collar, turn, 3ch, 1dc into first dc on previous row, * 2ch, 1dc into every second dc on previous row; rep from * to end. Press seams.

AMELIA, VERSIONS 2 & 3
Work Front as for Version 1 front from * to *.
Now refer to Amelia Graph B, appropriate colour key, and work in st st with colour changes and in repeat until 108(114,120) graph rows are completed.
Now cont working from graph, work as for Version 1 front from ** to end.
Work back as for front, omitting front neck shaping and working back neck shaping as for front Version 1.
Work sleeves & making up as for Version 1.

AMELIA Versions 1,2 & 3, Sleeve Graph

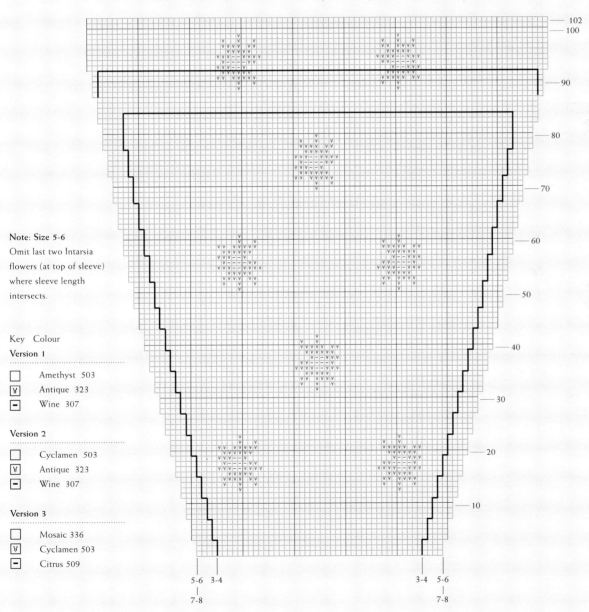

Note: Size 5-6
Omit last two Intarsia flowers (at top of sleeve) where sleeve length intersects.

Key Colour
Version 1

	Amethyst 503
V	Antique 323
−	Wine 307

Version 2

	Cyclamen 503
V	Antique 323
−	Wine 307

Version 3

	Mosaic 336
V	Cyclamen 503
−	Citrus 509

LUCY LOU

This plain or patterned sweater features bobble edging on the cuff, collar and band.
The patterned versions have a striped bodice and Lazy Daisy embroidered flowers on the sleeve. Both the plain and patterned versions are suitable for the **beginner knitter**.

Version 1

Version 2

Version 3

Version 4

Version 5

YARN
Jo Sharp 8 ply DK Pure Wool
Hand Knitting Yarn.

Code	Colour	Quantity x 50g balls		
Version 1		5-6	(7-8	9-10)
A	Forest 318	4	4	4
B	Lilac 324	2	2	2
C	Aegean 504	2	2	2
D	Mulberry 325	1	1	1
E	Mosiac 336	2	2	2
F	Jade 316	1	1	2
Version 2		5-6	(7-8	9-10)
A	Ink 901	3	3	4
B	Storm 706	2	2	2
C	Orchard 906	1	2	2
D	Heron 802	1	1	1
E	Embers 804	2	2	2
F	Miro 507	1	1	2
Version 3		5-6	(7-8	9-10)
A	Amethyst 503	6	7	7
Version 4		5-6	(7-8	9-10)
A	Black 302	6	7	7
Version 5		5-6	(7-8	9-10)
A	Cherry 309	6	7	7

MEASUREMENTS
(Measurements given in ins are approx.)

Sizes		
5-6	(7-8	9-10)
To fit chest		
62-66	67-71	72-76	cm
24½-26	26½-28	28¼-30	in
Bodice circumference		
82	86	90	cm
32¼	34	35½	in
Bodice length		
48	52	56	cm
19	20½	22	in
Sleeve length		
35	38.5	40.5	cm
13¾	15¼	16	in

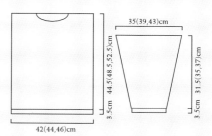

35(39,43)cm

44.5(48.5,52.5)cm

3.5cm

42(44,46)cm

31.5(35,37)cm

3.5cm

NEEDLES
1 pair 3.75mm needles (USA 5) (UK 9)
1 pair 4.50mm needles (USA 7) (UK 7)

TENSION
19.5 sts and 26 rows measured over 10cm
(approx 4″) st st using 4.50mm needles.

ABBREVIATIONS
Make Bobble (MB) K1,p1,k1,p1,k1 in next st
(5sts made), pass 1st,2nd,3rd and 4th sts over last
st made.

COLOUR SEQUENCES
Bodice, Versions 1 & 2
Working in st st.
Rows 1-2 col B, **Row 3** col C, **Row 4** col B,
Row 5 col D, **Row 6** col A, **Row 7** col E,
Row 8 col F, **Rows 9 - 11** col A.
Repeat these 11 rows throughout.

Sleeves, Versions 1 & 2
Working in st st
Rows 1 - 4 col A, **Rows 5** col C, **Row 6** col F,
Row 7 col C, **Rows 8 - 11** col A,
Rows 12 - 17 col E.
Rep rows 1 - 17.

VERSION 1
FRONT
Using 3.75mm needles and col A, cast on
82(86,90)sts. **Knit 5 rows. Purl 1 row.
Bobble Row (RS) K2,*MB, k3; rep from * to end.
Purl 1 row. Knit 4 rows.
Change to 4.50mm needles**.
Now work in Colour Sequence (above) until front
bodice (incl.band) measures 40.5(44.5,48.5)cm,
ending on a WS row.
Shape neck (RS) Work 35(37,39)sts, turn and
leave rem 47(49,51)sts on a holder.
Work each side of neck separately.
Dec 1st at beg (neck edge) on every row, 4 times,
then every foll alt row, 4 times [27(29,31)sts]
(13 shaping rows). Work 3 rows straight.
Shape Shoulders (RS) Cast off 9(10,10)sts at beg
next and foll alt rows once. Work 1 row. Cast off
rem 9(9,11)sts.

Leave 12 centre sts on holder. Rejoin yarn to rem
sts. Work second side to match first side, rev all
shaping.

BACK
Work back bodice to match front bodice, omitting
neck shaping and working shoulder shaping into
last 6 rows as follows;
Shape Shoulders Cast off 9(10,10)sts at beg next
4 rows, then 9(9,11)sts at beg next 2 rows.
Cast off rem 28 sts.

SLEEVES
Using 3.75mm needles and col A, cast on
38(42,46)sts. Work as for front from ** to **.
Shape sleeve Now working in colour sequence
for sleeves, AT THE SAME TIME inc 1st each end
next row, then 1st each end foll 5th rows,
10(11,13)times, then foll 6th rows 4(5,5)times
[68(76,84)sts] [75(86,95)shaping rows].
Work 7(5,1)rows straight. Cast off.

MAKING UP
Embroider sleeves Using cols B, C & D, embroider Lazy Daisys onto sleeves (as illustrated in
colour pages at front of book) using col F for centres of flowers.
Press all pieces gently on WS with a warm iron
over a damp cloth. Using Backstitch, join right
shoulder seams.
Neckband With RS facing, using 3.75mm needles
and col A, pick up and knit 18(20,22)sts along left
front, 12 sts from stitch holder at centre front,
18(20,22)sts along right front and 26 sts across
back neck [74(78,82)sts].
Knit 4 rows. Purl 1 row.
Bobble Row (RS) K2,* MB, k3; rep from * to end.
Purl 1 row. Knit 4 rows. Cast off. Join neckband
seam and left shoulder. Centre sleeves and join.
Join side and sleeve seams. Press seams.

VERSION 2
Work as for Version 1, substituting colours as per
colour key for Version 2.

VERSIONS 3, 4 & 5
Work as for Versions 1 & 2, using colour A
throughout.

LEONORA

The base garment for this fringed vest uses a slip stitch pattern. Once the base garment is created, the shaggy finish is added using columns of Stocking stitch which are sewn onto the garment, then cut and frayed. This garment is suitable for an **average skilled knitter**.

Version 1

Version 2

YARN

Jo Sharp 8 ply DK Pure Wool
Hand Knitting Yarn.

No.	Colour	Quantity x 50g balls		
Version 1		5-6	(7-8)	9-10
A	Ebony 902	5	6	7
B	Gold 320	1	1	1
C	Pistachio 002	1	1	1
D	Tangerine 003	1	1	1
Version 2		5-6	(7-8	9-10)
A	Cyclamen 006	8	9	10

NEEDLES

1 pair 5.00mm needles (USA 8) (UK 6)
1 pair 3.25mm needles (USA 3) (UK 10)
1 3.50mm crochet hook.

TENSION

26 stitches and 40 rows measured over 10cm (approx. 4") of Woven stitch pattern using 5.00mm needles.

WOVEN STITCH PATTERN

Row 1(RS) K1* yf, sl1 purlwise, yb, k1, rep from * to end.
Row 2 (WS) P2 * yb, sl1 purlwise, yf, p1, rep from * to last st, p1.

BACK

Using 5.00mm needles and col A, cast on 111(123,131)sts.
*Working in Woven stitch, patt until back (from beg) measures 19(20,21)cm, ending on a WS row.**
Shape armholes (RS) Cast off 6(8,10)sts at beg next 2 rows. Dec 1st at each end of next row, then foll alt rows 6 times [85(93,97)sts] (15 shaping rows). Continue working straight until back (from beg) measures 34(36,38)cm, ending on a WS row.
Shape shoulders (RS) Cast off 9(11,12)sts at beg next 4 rows, then 10sts at beg next 2 rows. Leave rem 29sts on holder.

LEFT FRONT

Using 5.00mm needles and col A, cast on 55(61,65)sts.
Work as for back from * to **.
Shape armhole (RS) Cast off 6(8,10)sts at beg next row, then dec 1st at beg foll alt rows, 7 times [42(46,48)sts]. Cont without shaping until work (from beg) measures 30(32,33)cm.

MEASUREMENTS

(Measurements given in inches are approximate)
Sizing

5-6	(7-8	9-10)	
To fit chest			
62 - 66	67 - 71	72 - 76	cm
24½ - 26	26½ - 28	28½ - 30	in
Bodice circumference			
82	92	98	cm
32¼	36¼	38½	in
Bodice length			
36	38	40	cm
14¼	15	15¾	cm

2cm
15(16,17)cm
19(20,21)cm
21(23,25)cm
42(47,50)cm

ending on a RS row.

Shape neck (WS) Cast off 6 sts at beg (neck edge) of next row, then 1st at on foll 8 rows [28(32,34)sts] (9 shaping rows).
Work 10 rows without shaping.
Shape shoulder (RS) Cast off 9(11,12)sts at beg next and foll alt row, work 1 row, then cast off rem 10 sts.

RIGHT FRONT

Work as for left front, rev all shaping.

MAKING UP

With wrong sides facing, using Edge to Edge stitch, join side and shoulder seams.

Collar With RS facing, using 5.00mm needles and col A, pick up and knit 26 sts up right front neck, 29sts from holder at back neck and 26sts down left front neck (81sts). Work 4cm in Woven stitch pattern. Cast off using a crochet hook .

Make first fringe column Using 3.25mm needles and col B, cast on 7sts.
*Row 1 (RS) K3, K1 tbl, K3.
Row 2 (WS) P3, P1 tbl, P3*.
Cont from * to * until length required, leave sts on a holder. Now cont in patt making as many columns in colour/s as desired to cover garment. Columns to run horizontally around bodice, as shown in illustration in colour pages at front of book.

Place columns Pin all knitted columns into place covering garment as desired, and leaving 1cm between each. (Note: a knitted column, once unravelled for fringing will extend beyond its original width). Use Backstitch to sew first column to garment through central st of each row, creating a stitch line along the centre of the column.
One Backstitch through the central st in each row of knitting holds fringe in place. Repeat for each column. Once all column lengths are secured, remove stitch holder from first column and using scissors, remove the first stitch from both sides of this column, along the entire length of the column. Then, starting from the top of the first column undo the next two sts on every row on each side to create the surface fringe effect. Cont same for all columns.

POPPY

A simple drop shoulder style tunic embelished with Stocking stitch cord on the hemline and bodice. The embroidery is easy to achieve for the novice embroiderer and the project is suitable for **a beginner knitter.**

Version 1   Version 2

YARN

Jo Sharp 8 ply DK Pure Wool Hand Knitting Yarn.

Code	Colour	Quantity x 50g balls		
Version 1		3-4	(5-6	7-8)
A	Owl 801	7	8	9
B	Cyclamen 006	1	1	1
C	Cherry 309	1	1	1
D	Coral 304	1	1	1
E	Gold 320	1	1	1
F	Chartreuse 330			
Version 2		3-4	(5-6	7-8)
A	Silk 903	7	8	9
B	Owl 801	1	1	1
C	Heron 802	1	1	1
D	Natural 301	1	1	1
E	Natural 301	allocated above		
F	Ginger 322	1	1	1

NEEDLES

1 pair 3.75mm needles (USA 5) (UK 9)
1 pair 4.00mm needles (USA 6) (UK 8)
1 set 3.75mm double pointed needles (USA 5) (UK 9)
1 set 3.75mm circular needles (USA 5) (UK 9)

See measurements & diagram on next page

Poppy, continued...

MEASUREMENTS

(Measurements given in inches are approximate)

Sizing

3-4	(5-6	7-8)	
To fit chest			
57 - 61	62 - 66	67 - 71	cm
22¹/₂ - 24	24¹/₂ - 26	26¹/₂ - 28	in
Bodice circumference			
76	86	96	cm
30	34	37³/₄	in
Bodice length			
40	45	50	cm
15³/₄	17³/₄	19³/₄	in
Sleeve length			
31	33	37	cm
12¹/₄	13	14¹/₂	in

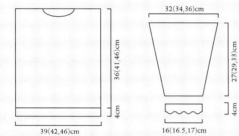

TENSION

22.5sts and 30 rows measured over 10cm
(approx. 4") of st st, using 4.00mm needles.

TO MAKE CORDS

Using 3.75mm double pointed needles and col A,
cast on 4 sts. *K4, do not turn work, slide sts to
right end of needle and pull yarn to tighten. Rep
from * for 10cm (approx 4"), leave sts on needle,
do not cast off.

BACK

Make 11(12,13) cords and hold tog on left needle.
K4 from 1st cord, *k4 from next cord on needle,
bring cast on edge of previous cord to the back of
cord just knit and pick up and knit 4 cast on sts,
rep from *, end by picking up and knitting the 4
cast on sts of last cord [88(96,104)sts].
Now working in Garter st (knit all rows), work
4cm ending on a WS row.
Change to 4.00mm needles. Working in st st,
beginning with a knit row (RS)*, work until back
measures 38(43,48)cm (incl. band, not loops)

ending on a WS row.
Shape back neck (RS) Knit 39(43,47)sts, turn,
leave rem 49(53,57)sts on holder. Work each side
of neck separately. Cast off 3 sts at neck edge on
next row then on foll alt row once, then 4(5,6)sts
on foll alt row once. Cast off rem 29(32,35)sts.
Rejoin yarn to rem sts. Cast off 10 centre sts. Work
second side to match first side, rev all shaping.

FRONT

Work as for back to *. Cont until front (incl. band, not
loops) measures 34(39,44)cm, ending on a WS row.
Shape neck (RS) Knit 39(43,47)sts, turn, leave
rem sts on holder.
Work each side of neck separately.
Cast off 2(3,3)sts at beg (neck edge) of next row,
then 2 sts on foll alt rows twice, then 1 st on
every row 4(5,5)times [29(31,35)sts]
[9(10,10)shaping rows].
Work 9(8,8)rows straight. Cast off. Cast off 10
centre sts. Work second side to match first side,
rev all shaping.

SLEEVES

Using 4.00mm needles, cast on 36(37,38)sts.
Shape sleeve Working in st st, inc 1 st at each end
of every 4th row 18(20,22)times. Work 7(9,11)rows
straight [72(77,82)sts] [81(87,99)rows].

SLEEVE EDGING

Using 3.75mm needles and col 1, cast on 7 sts.
Knit 1 row.
Row 1 K5, k into front and back of next st, k1 (8sts).
Row 2 K1, k into front and back of next st, k6 (9sts).
Row 3 K7, k into front and back of next st, k1 (10sts).
Row 4 K1, k into front and back of next st, k8 (11sts).
Row 5 K9, k into front and back of next st, k1 (12sts).
Row 6 K1, k into front and back of next st, k10 (13sts).
Row 7 K11, k into front and back of next st, k1 (14sts).
Row 8 K1, k into front and back of next st, k12 (15sts).
Row 9 K12, k2 tog, k1 (14sts).
Row 10 K1, k2 tog, k11 (13sts).
Row 11 K10, k2 tog, k1 (12sts).
Row 12 K1, k2tog, k9 (11sts).

Row 13 K8, k2 tog, k1 (10sts).
Row 14 K1, k2tog, k7 (9sts).
Row 15 K6, k2 tog, k1 (8sts).
Row 16 K1, k2tog, k5 (7sts).
Repeat rows 1 - 16 until length measures
16(16.5,17)cm. Cast off.

MAKING UP
Press all pieces gently on WS using a warm iron
over a damp cloth.
Embroidery Refer to colour illustrations in front
section of book for placement of embroidery and
to diagram below for large flower motifs.
Note: To make evenly shaped circles of embroidery for large flowers, tack a circle as a guide
before beginning embroidery.
Full or Half strands Embroidery uses either a full
or half strand of yarn. To make a half strand,
divide the 4 ends of yarn into two sets of two

strands each, and pull apart.
Leaves on flower stalks Using a full strand
embroider in Lazy Daisy stitch with (col F for
Version 1 and col D for Version 2).
Small Daisys Embroider 6 daisys on each sleeve
and 8 daisys on front bodice using a full strand
and col B for petals and a half strand and col F for
centres .
Sew together Using Backstitch, join shoulder
seams. Centre sleeves and join. Join side and
sleeve seams, using Edge to Edge stitch on bands.
Sew sleeve edging onto sleeves, using Edge to
Edge stitch, leaving sleeve edge seams open.
Neckband With RS facing, using 3.75mm circular
needle and col A, pick up and knit 22(23,24)sts
down left front, 10 sts at centre front, 22(23,24)sts
up right front, 32(34,36)sts across back neck
[86(90,94)sts]. Work 12 rounds in Garter st
(round 1 knit, round 2 purl etc.) Cast off.

COLOUR KEY

Version 1

Code	Colour
A	Owl 801
B	Cyclamen 006
C	Cherry 309
D	Coral 304
E	Gold 320
F	Chartreuse 330

Version 2

Code	Colour
A	Silk 903
B	Owl 801
C	Heron 802
D	Natural 301
E	Natural 301
F	Ginger 322

ABBREVIATIONS KEY
(fs) = full strand
(hs) = half strand

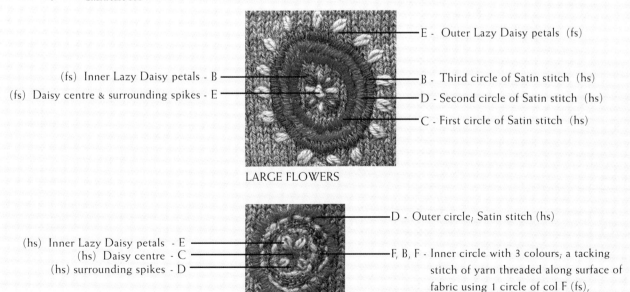

E - Outer Lazy Daisy petals (fs)
(fs) Inner Lazy Daisy petals - B
B - Third circle of Satin stitch (hs)
(fs) Daisy centre & surrounding spikes - E
D - Second circle of Satin stitch (hs)
C - First circle of Satin stitch (hs)

LARGE FLOWERS

D - Outer circle; Satin stitch (hs)
(hs) Inner Lazy Daisy petals - E
(hs) Daisy centre - C
F, B, F - Inner circle with 3 colours; a tacking
(hs) surrounding spikes - D
stitch of yarn threaded along surface of
fabric using 1 circle of col F (fs),
3 circles col B (hs), 1 circle col F (fs)

SMALL FLOWERS

MATILDA

This drop shoulder sweater is bordered with a cable fringe and features an easy to knit slip stitch sleeve. Versions 1 & 2 have a colourful Intarsia (picture) technique on the bodice, suitable for an **experienced knitter** with knowledge of **Intarsia technique**. Version 3 is worked in a single colour throughout and is a suitable project for an **average knitter**.

Version 1

Version 2

Version 3

YARN

Jo Sharp 8 ply DK Pure Wool
Hand Knitting Yarn.

Code	Key	Colour	Quantity x 50g balls		
Version 1			3-4	(5-6	7-8)
A	+	Tangerine 003	2	2	2
B	•	Cyclamen 006	1	1	1
C	−	Aegean 504	1	2	2
D	×	Chatreuse 330	1	1	1
E	◣	Wine 307	1	1	2
F	☐	Cherry 309	4	5	6
G	▯	Mosaic 336	1	1	1

Code	Key	Colour			
Version 2			3-4	(5-6	7-8)
A	×	Mosaic 336	1	1	1
B	−	Wine 307	1	2	2
C	▯	Ruby 326	1	1	1
D	◣	Antique 323	1	1	2
E	•	Ginger 322	1	1	1
F	☐	Teal 007	5	6	7
G	+	Summer 001	1	1	1

Version 3		3-4	(5-6	7-8)	
A		Ebony 902	7	8	9

NEEDLES

1 pair 3.75mm needles (USA 5) (UK 9)
1 pair 4.00mm needles (USA 6) (UK 8)
1 pair 3.75mm circular needle (USA 5) (UK 9)

TENSION

Measured over 10cm (approx. 4″) using 4.00mm needles.
Bodice 22.5sts and 30rows in st st and Intarsia.
Sleeve 22.5sts and 33rows in Texture Pattern.

MEASUREMENTS

(Measurements given in inches are approximate)
Sizing

3-4	(5-6	7-8)	
To fit chest			
57 - 61	62 - 66	67 - 71	cm
22½ - 24	24½ - 26	26½ - 28	in
Bodice circumference			
76	82	90	cm
30	32¼	35½	in
Bodice length			
45	50	53	cm
17¾	19¾	21	in
Sleeve length			
31	34	37	cm
12¼	13½	14½	in

See next page for Measurement Diagram

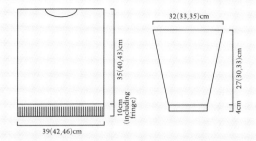

BACK

Using 4.00mm needles and col F, cast on 88(96,104)sts. Working in st st & intarsia through-out, refer to graph for pattern placement and colour changes (or work in col A throughout for version 3) *.

Cont until 100(114,124)graph rows have been worked.

Shape back neck (RS) Knit 39(43,47)sts, turn, leave rem 49(53,57)sts on holder. Work each side of neck separately. Cast off 3 sts at beg (neck edge) of next row, then on foll alt row once, then 4(5,5)sts on foll alt row once.

Cast off rem 29(32,36)sts. Rejoin yarn to rem sts. Place 10 centre sts on holder. Work second side as first side, rev all shaping.

FRONT

Work as for back to *. Cont until 88(100,112)rows have been worked.

Shape neck (RS) Knit 39(43,47)sts, turn, leave rem 49(53,57)sts on holder. Work each side of neck separately. Cast off 2 sts at beg (neck edge) of next row, then 2sts on foll alt rows twice, then 1 st on every row, 4(5,5)times [29(32,36)sts] [98(111,123)graph rows]. Work 8(9,7)rows straight. Cast off. Place 10 centre sts on holder. Work second side to match first side, rev all shaping.

TEXTURE PATTERN FOR SLEEVE

Multiple 4+3
Note: use col A throughout for Version 3.
Special Abbreviations
wyif - with yarn in front
wyib - with yarn in back
Note: slip all slip sts purlwise.

Keep pattern correct on rows 17-22 and 41-46, allowing for increases.

Rows 1 & 2 col A, **Row 3** col B
Rows 4 - 6 col C.
Row 7 col D, P3 * K1, p3; rep from * to end.
Row 8 col E, **Rows 9 - 11** col C
Row 12 col B, **Rows 13 & 14** col A
Rows 15 & 16 col F
Row 17 col E, K3 * wyib sl1, k3; rep from * to end.
Row 18 col E, K3 * wyif sl1, k3; rep from * to end.
Row 19 col C, K1 * wyib sl1, k3; rep from * to end.
Row 20 col C, K1 * wyif sl1, k3; rep from * to end.
Row 21 col D as row 17.
Row 22 col D, P1, k1, p1 * wyif sl1, p1, k1, p1; rep from * to end.
Rows 23 & 24 col F, **Rows 25 & 26** col E
Row 27 col C, **Rows 28 - 30** col B
Row 31 col A, as row 7, **Row 32** col E
Rows 33 - 35 col B, **Row 36** col C
Rows 37 & 38 col E, **Rows 39 & 40** col D
Row 41 col F, as row 17
Row 42 col F, as row 18
Row 43 col E, as row 19
Row 44 col E, as row 20
Row 45 col B, as row 17
Row 46 col B, as row 22
Row 47 col D, **Row 48** col D
Rows 1 - 48 Form pattern repeat.

SLEEVE

Note: use col A throughout for Version 3.
Using 3.75mm needles and col A, cast on 33(36,39)sts.

Row 1 (RS) * K3, k1, p1, k1; rep from * to end.
Row 2 * K1, p1, k1, p3; rep from * to end.
These 2 rows form pattern.
Row 3 Change to col F and cont in patt until work (from beg) measures 4cm, inc 2(3,4)sts across last WS row [35(39,43)sts].
Change to 4.00mm needles.
Shape Sleeve (RS) Now working in Texure Pattern repeat throughout, beg on row 1 (RS), AT THE SAME TIME inc 1st at each end of every 4th row 19(13,10)times, then every 5th row 0(6,10)times. [73(77,83)sts] [76(82,90)shaping rows]. Work 4(8,8)rows straight. Cast off.

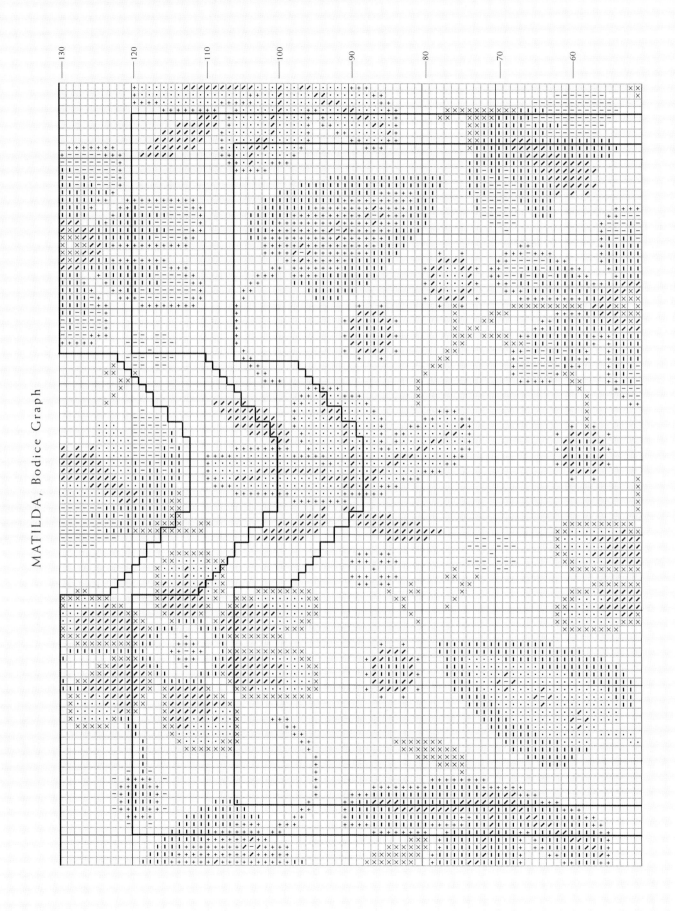

MATILDA, Bodice Graph

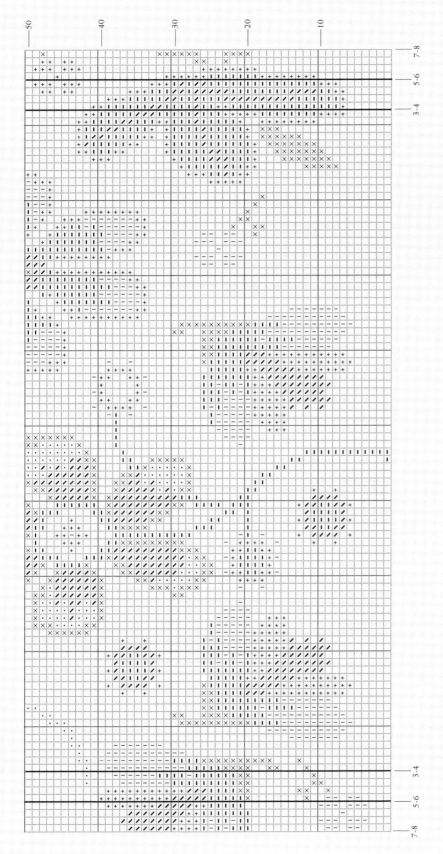

MAKING UP

Note: use col A throughout for version 3.
Press all pieces gently on WS, using a warm
iron over a damp cloth. Using Backstitch,
join shoulder seams. Centre sleeves and join,
join side and sleeve seams.

Neckband With RS facing, using 3.75mm
circular needle and col F, pick up and knit
23sts down left front neck, 10sts from holder
at centre front, 23sts up right front and 40sts
across back neck (96sts).
Work in rounds as follows;
Round 1 * K4, p1, k1; rep from * to end.
Round 2 * K3, p1,k1, p1; rep from * to end.
Repeat rounds 1 & 2, 4 times (10 rounds).
Change to col E, work a further 2 rounds,
cast off.

FRINGED BAND

Using 3.75mm needles and (colour A,
Version 1) or (colour F, Version 2) cast on 13 sts.
Foundation row (WS) [K5,p1] 2 times, k1.
Row 1 (RS) P1, k1b, p2, ([k1, k1b, yo] 2
times, k1, k1b) in same st, p2, k1b, k5
(20sts).
Row 2 K5, p1b, k2, p8, k2, p1b, k1.
Row 3 P1, k1b, p2, k6, k2tog, p2, k1b, k5
(19sts).
Row 4 K5, p1b, k2, p7, k2, p1b, k1.
Row 5 P1, k1b, p2, k5, k2tog, p2, k1b, k5
(18sts).
Row 6 K5, p1b, k2, p6, k2, p1b, k1.
Row 7 P1, k1b, p2, k4, k2tog, p2, k1b, k5
(17sts).
Row 8 K5, p1b, k2, p5, k2, p1b, k1.
Row 9 P1, k1b, p2, k3, k2tog, p2, k1b, k5
(16sts).
Row 10 K5, p1b, k2, p4, k2, p1b, k1.
Row 11 P1, k1b, p2, k2, k2tog, p2, k1b, k5
(15sts).
Row 12 K5, p1b, k2, p3, k2, p1b, k1.

MATILDA, Making up, continued...

Row 13 P1, k1b, p2, k1, k2tog, p2, k1b, k5 (14sts).
Row 14 K5, p1b, k2, p2, k2, p1b, k1.
Row 15 P1, k1b, p2, k2tog, p2, k1b, k5 (13 sts).
Row 16 K 5, p1b, k2, p1, k2, p1b, k1.
Rep rows 1-16 for desired length, sewing into place as you go (stretching slightly) and ending on a WS row.

With RS facing, cast off 8sts, cut yarn and pull tail through rem sts on right needle. Slip rem sts off left needle and unravel them on every row.

Twist fringe Gently roll each loop between thumb and first finger until the required twist is achieved; slip twist onto a knitting needle to hold in place. Steam lightly to set twist.

PHOEBE'S BAG

This little shoulder bag is made using a slip stitch pattern which creates a very flat fabric. It is then embellished with crochet flowers or jewels which are sewn or glued in place . This project is suitable for a **beginner knitter.**

Version 1   Version 2

WOVEN STITCH

Multiple 2+1
Row 1 (RS) K1,*yf, sl1 purlwise, yb, k1; rep from * to end.
Row 2 P2,*yb, sl1 purlwise, yf, p1; rep from * to last st, p1.
Rep these 2 rows.

NEEDLES

1 pair 5.00mm needles (USA 8) (UK 6)
1 x 4.00mm crochet hook (Version 1)

TENSION

26sts and 44rows measured over 10cm (approx. 4")
Woven stitch, using 5.00mm needles.

MEASUREMENTS

(Measurements given in inches are approx.)

Bag width	20 cm	8 in
Bag depth	25 cm	9³/4 in
Strap length	70 cm	27¹/2 in
Strap width	8 cm	3¹/4 in

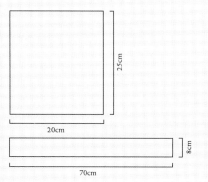

YARN

Jo Sharp 8 ply DK Pure Wool
Hand Knitting Yarn.

Code	Colour	Quantity
Version 1		x 50g balls
A	Renaissance 312	3
B	Cherry 309	1
C	Coral 304	1
D	Jade 316	1
E	Wine 307	1

(note: each flower motif uses approx 3 metres of yarn)

Version 2		
A	Cherry 309	3

JEWELS

For Version 2, assorted jewels.

BAG PATTERN

Using 5.00mm needles and col A, cast on 65sts.
Row 1 Work 65sts in Woven stitch, turn, leave a 30cm loop of yarn before continuing across Row 2. Cont working this way, leaving a loop of yarn at one edge until piece measures 20cm. Now cont working straight (without leaving loop) until piece measures 40cm from beg. Cast off.
Strap Using 5.00mm needles and col A, cast on 21sts. Work in Woven stitch until piece measures 70cm. Cast off.

MAKING UP

Strap Fold strap lengthwise with RS facing, using Backstitch, sew seam. Turn RS out and press.
Bag Fold main piece in half with RS facing, using Backstitch, sew side seam, leaving fringing at bottom. Turn RS out and press.
Hold bag so that back of bag (the half without fringing) is facing up. Using overstitch, sew the bottom edge of the back of bag to just above the fringe on the front. Make sure that stitching leaves the fringe hanging free. Sew the two ends of strap to sides of bag.
Make fringes Trim ends of fringe, tie in bunches of 4-6 strands.
Make motifs for Version 1
Refer to page 1 for crochet abbreviations.
Using a 4.00mm crochet hook and col B, Make 2
Flower Motifs; *Ch 5 and join a ring with sl st.
Round 1 14 dc in ring.
Round 2 2 dc, 1 leaf [ch 4, (yrh twice, insert hook in next st, draw up a loop, yrh, draw through 2 loops, yrh, draw through 2 loops) 3 times in same st, yrh draw through 4 loops, ch 3], 1 dc in each of next 2 sts, 4 more leaves as above, fasten off *. Repeat from * using cols C, D & E, completing 8 motifs in all.
Decorate Versions 1 & 2
Refer to colour illustrations in front pages of book to decorate.
For Version 1, sew on crochet motifs and for Version 2, arrange jewels and either sew or glue in place.

BLOSSOM CAP

This project is suitable for a **beginner knitter.**

YARN

Jo Sharp 8 ply DK Pure Wool
Hand Knitting Yarn.

No.	Colour	Quantity x 50g balls.
A	Wine 307	2
B	Cherry 309	1
C	Coral 304	1

Note: Each flower uses approx 3.5metres of yarn.

NEEDLES

1 pair 3.75mm needles (USA 5) (UK 9)
1 pair 4.50mm needles (USA 7) (UK 7)
1 x 4.00mm crochet hook

MEASUREMENTS

(Measurements given in inches are approximate)

Hat	One size fits All
Circumference	47cm (18¹/₂")

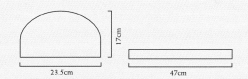

17cm   23.5cm   47cm

TENSION

22.5 sts and 30 rows measured over 10cm (approx 4") st st using 4.00mm needles.

CAP

Using 3.75mm needles, cast on 107 sts. Work 4 rows Garter st (knit all rows). Change to 4.00mm needles and work 8cm st st. Now work as for Navy Beanie (p 47) from ** to **.
Brim Using 3.75mm needles, cast on 137 sts. Knit 1 row.

Blossom Cap, continued...

Next row [Knit 12 sts, dec 1 st) 10 times, knit to end (127 sts).
Knit 1 row.
Next row [Knit 11 sts, dec 1 st)10 times, knit to end (117 sts).
Knit 1 row.

Next row [Knit 10 sts, dec 1 st)10 times, knit to end (107 sts). Knit 1 row. Cast off loosely.
Using Edge to Edge st, sew brim to cap.
Decorate Cap Crochet 3 Flower motifs (as per previous pattern, Pheobe's Bag). Make one blossom in each of cols A, B & C, and sew in place as per colour illustration in front pages of book.

AUBERGINE BERET

This project is suitable for a **beginner knitter**.

YARN

Jo Sharp 8 ply DK Pure Wool
Hand Knitting Yarn.

Colour	Quantity x 50g balls.
Aubergine 008	1

NEEDLES

1 pair 4.00mm needles (USA 6) (UK 8)
1 pair 4.50mm needles (USA 7) (UK 7)

MEASUREMENTS

(Measurements given in inches are approximate)

One size fits all

Circumference	39cm (15½")

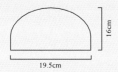

TENSION

22.5 sts and 30 rows measured over 10cm (approx 4") st st using 4.00mm needles.

MOSS STITCH

Row 1 (RS) K1, p1 to end.
Row 2 (WS) K the p sts and P the k sts as they face you.
Rows 1 & 2 form Moss stitch pattern.

BERET

Using 4.00mm needles, cast on 84 sts and work 7 rows k2, p2 rib, increasing 1 st in last WS row.
Next row (RS) (k1, p1, k1, m1)28 times, k1 (113 sts).
Change to 4.50mm needles.
Working in Moss st (beg with k1) work 9 rows.
Shape top
Row 1 (RS) (K8, m1)14 times, k1 (127sts).
Next row (WS) Purl
Work 8 rows st st.
Row 11 (RS) (K7, k2tog)14 times, k1 (113 sts).
Work 3 rows st st.
Row 15 (RS) (K13, k3tog)7 times, k1 (99 sts).
Work 3 rows st st.
Row 19 (RS) (K11, k3tog)7 times, k1 (85 sts).
Work 3 rows st st.
Row 23 (RS) (K9, k3tog)7 times, k1 (71 sts).
Work 3 rows st st.
Row 27 (RS) (K7, k3tog)7 times, k1 (57 sts).
Work 1 row st st.
Row 29 (RS) (K5, k3tog)7 times, k1 (43 sts).
Row 30 (RS) P1 (p3tog, p3)7 times, p1 (29sts).
Row 31 (RS) (K1, k3tog)7 times, k1 (15 sts).
Break yarn and thread through 15 rem sts, pull thread tightly & secure. Sew seam using Edge to Edge stitch.

MOSS STITCH BEANIE

This project is suitable for a **beginner knitter**.

Version 1   Version 2

YARN

Jo Sharp 8 ply DK Pure Wool
Hand Knitting Yarn.

Colour	Quantity
Version 1	x 50g balls
Natural 301	2
Version 2	
Storm 706	2

NEEDLES

1 pair 3.75mm needles (USA 5) (UK 9)

MEASUREMENTS

(Measurements given in inches are approximate)

One size fits All

Circumference   47cm (18½")

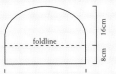

TENSION

22.5 sts and 30 rows measured over 10cm
(approx 4") st st using 4.00mm needles.

MOSS STITCH

Row 1 (RS) K1, p1.
Row 2 (WS) Knit the purl sts and purl the knit sts,
as they face you.
Rows 1 & 2 form pattern.

BEANIE

Using 3.75mm needles, cast on 107 sts and work
8cm in Moss st, ending on a WS row.
Change to 4.00mm needles.
Now work in st st until work (from beg) measures
16cm. Now work as for Navy Beanie (below)
from ** to **. Fold back brim.

NAVY BEANIE

This project is suitable for a **beginner knitter**.

YARN

Jo Sharp 8 ply DK
Pure Wool Hand
Knitting Yarn.

Colour	Quantity
	x 50g balls
Navy 327	2

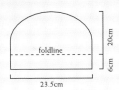

MEASUREMENTS

(Measurements given in
inches are approximate)

One size fits all
Circumference   47cm (18½")

NEEDLES

1 pair 3.75mm needles (USA 5) (UK 9)

TENSION

22.5 sts and 30 rows measured over 10cm
(approx 4") st st using 4.00mm needles.

BEANIE

Using 3.75mm needles, cast on 107sts.
Row 1 *P2, k2, rep from * to last st, p1.
Row 2 * K2, p2, rep from * to last st, k1.
Rep rows 1 & 2 until 6cm are completed, ending
on a RS row. Change to 4.00mm needles. Now
work in st st until 20cm have been worked, ending
on a WS row.

Navy Beanie, continued...

Shape top Row 1 (RS) K1, k2tog, [k23, k3tog tbl]3 times, k23, k2tog tbl, k1 (99sts).
Purl one row.
Row 3 K1, k2otg, [k21,k3tog tbl]3times, k21, k2tog tbl, k1 (91sts).
Purl 1 row.
Row 5 K1, k2otg, [k19, k3tog tbl]3times, k19,

k2tog tbl, k1 (83sts).
Purl 1 row. Cont decreasing 8 sts in each RS row until 43sts rem.
Next row (WS) P1, p2tog tbl, [p7, p3tog tbl]3 times, p7, p2tog, p1 (35sts).
Cont decreasing 8 sts every row until 11 sts rem. Break yarn and thread through 11 rem sts, pull thread tightly & secure. Sew seam using Edge to Edge stitch. ** Fold back brim.

SASHA'S SCARF

This striped, ribbed scarf is a suitable project for a **beginner knitter.**

Version 1   Version 2

YARN
Jo Sharp 8 ply DK Pure Wool
Hand Knitting Yarn.

Code	Colour	Quantity
Version 1		x 50g balls
A	Cherry 309	1
B	Cyclamen 006	1
C	Chartreuse 330	1
D	Amethyst 503	2
E	Summer 001	1
F	Silk 903	1
G	Heron 802	1

Code	Colour	Quantity
Version 2		
A	Aubergine 008	1
B	Cyclamen 006	1
C	Tangerine 003	1
D	Plum 505	2
E	Chartreuse 330	1
F	Renaissance 312	1
G	Jade 316	1

MEASUREMENTS
(Measurements given in inches are approx.)

Width	14 cm	(5½ in)
Length	120 cm	(47¼ in)

14cm
120cm

NEEDLES
1 pair 3.75mm needles (USA 5) (UK 9)

TENSION
41.5 sts and 28 rows measured over 10cm (approx. 4") of k2, p2 rib, using 3.75mm needles.

SCARF
Using 3.75mm needles and col A, cast on 58 sts.
Now work in k2, p2 rib as follows;
Rows 1 - 4 col A, **Rows 5 - 8** col B,
Rows 9 & 10 col C, **Rows 11 & 12** col D,
Row 13 col E, **Rows 14 - 16** col D,
Rows 17 & 18 col F, **Rows 19 & 20** col G.
Repeat rows 1 - 20 in patt until work measures 120cm or to desired length.
Cast off.
Sew in ends neatly.

JO SHARP

Hand Knitting Collection Stockists

AUSTRALIA
Head Office & Mail Order Enquiries
JO SHARP HAND KNITTING YARN
PO Box 357 Albany WA 6331 Australia
Telephone +61 08 9842 2250 Facsimile +61 08 9842 2260
email - yarn@josharp.com.au   website - www.josharp.com.au

New South Wales

Champion Textiles	Newtown	02 9519 6677
Greta's Handcraft Centre	Lindfield	02 9416 2489
Hand to Hand Crafts	Newcastle	02 4929 7255
Hornsby Wool & Craft Nook	Hornsby	02 9482 4924
Inca Wool Shed	Turramurra	02 9440 9111
Jimana Crafts	Long Jetty	02 4332 1307
Knit It	Beecroft	02 9875 5844
Katoomba Knit. & Needlecraft	Katoomba	02 4782 6137
Phebe's Gift & Homewares	Eastwood	02 9874 7867
Pins and Needles	Merimbula	02 6495 3646
Sue's Cherryhills	Pennant Hills	02 9484 0212
Sheep's Back Wool Gallery	Yass	02 6226 3072
Tapestry Crafts	Sydney	02 9299 3470
The Armidale Wool Shop	Armidale	02 6772 7083
The Wool Inn	Penrith	02 4732 2201
The Wool Room	Young	02 6383 3254

Australian Capital Territory

Shearing Shed	Manuka	02 6295 0061
Stitch 'n Time	Mawson	02 6286 4378

Queensland

Cooroy Drapery	Cooroy	07 5447 6145
Craftnits	Gympie	07 5482 6190
Heirloom Creations	Toowoomba	07 4639 2201
Rosemary's Wool & Craft	Nambour	07 5441 1744
Threads & More	Bardon	07 3371 5835

Tasmania

Needle 'n' Thread	Devonport	03 6424 6920
Tasmanian Wool Suppliers	Moonah	03 6278 1800
The Spinning Wheel	Hobart	03 6234 1711

South Australia

Highgate Needle Nook	Highgate	08 8271 4670
Needles 'N' Yarns	Berri	08 8582 1111
The Bay Window	Kingscote	08 8553 2740
Wildwood Arts & Crafts	Woodside	08 8389 7500

Victoria

Bacchus Marsh Wool Shop	Bacchus Marsh	03 5367 1514
Knitters of Australia	Hampton	03 9533 1233
Knitters of Australia	Surrey Hills	03 9836 9614
Knitting & Sewing Centre	Colac	03 5231 3152
Kyabram Toyworld	Kyabram	03 5852 2862
Mansfield Craft Den	Mansfield	03 5775 2044
	www.craftden.com.au	
Melton Drapery	Melton	03 9743 5484
Mooroolbark Craft & Habby	Mooroolbark	03 9726 7291
Sunbury Wool Centre	Sunbury	03 9744 4520
Sunspun	Canterbury	03 9830 1609
The Stitchery	Essendon	03 9379 9790
	www.stitchery.com.au	
Uniform & Wool Centre	Warnambool	03 5562 9599
Wool Village	Mulgrave	03 9560 5869

Western Australia

Boolah Art & Craft Supplies	Albany	08 9842 1042
Crossway's Wool & Fabrics	Subiaco	08 9381 4286
	www.woolshop.com.au	
Ivy and Maude	Cottesloe	08 9384 4225
The Little Daisy Craft Studio	Morley	08 9375 1135
The Wool Shack	Innaloo	08 9446 6344

NEW ZEALAND Mail Order Enquiries
Knit-a-Holics Unlimited / PO Box 30645, Lower Hutt, NZ
Ph. 04 586 4530 Fax 04 586 4531
email: knitting@xtra.co.nz

Creative Fashion Centre	Lower Hutt	04 566 4689
	Tawa	04 232 8088
Knit World	Auckland	09 837 6111
	Palmerston North	06 356 8974
	New Plymouth	06 758 3171
	Christchurch	03 379 2300
	Hastings	06 878 0090
	Dunedin	03 477 0400
	Wellington	04 385 1918
	Hamilton	07 838 3868
Knit'n'Save	Levin	06 367 9700

CANADA Wholesale Enquiries - Estelle Designs
Units 65/67 2220 Midland Ave. Scarborough, Ontario M1P 3E6
Telephone 416 298 9922 - Facsimile 416 298 2429
www.estelledesigns.ca

Canadian Retail Stores

Alberta

Wool Revival	Edmonton	780 471 2749

British Columbia

Boutique de Laine	Victoria	250 592 9616
Touch of Wool	Vancouver	604 224 9276
Neverending Yarn	Vernon	250-545-0972

Manitoba

Ram Wools	Winnipeg	204 949 6868
	www.ramwools.com	
The Sheep Boutique	Winnipeg	204 786 8887

Ontario

Christina Tandberg Knits	London	519 672 4088
Elizabeth's Wool Shop	Kitchener	519 744 1881
Knit or Knot	Aurora	905 713 1818
London Yarns & Machines	London	519 474 0403
Myrtle Station Wool Studio	Ashburn	905 655 4858
Needles and Knits	Aurora	905 713 2066
Passionknit Ltd	Toronto	416 322 0688
Romni Wools	Toronto	416 703 0202
The Knitting Habit	Niagara Falls	905 357 9730
The Needle Emporium	Ancaster	905 648 1994
	www.needleemporium.com	
The Yarn Tree	Streetsville	905 821 3170
Village Yarns	Toronto	416 232 2361
	www.villageyarns.com	
Wool-Tyme	Nepean	613 225 WOOL
	www.wooltyme.com	
Cloth & Clay	Waterloo	519-886-7400

U.S.A., Wholesale Enquiries - Classic Elite Yarns
300A Jackson Street Lowell, MA 01852
Telephone 978 453 2837 - Facsimile 978 452 3085

U.S.A. Retail Stores

Alabama

Yarn Expressions	Huntsville	800-283-8409
	knit@yarnexpressions.com	
	www.YarnExpressions.com	

Alaska

Net Loft (Seasonal)	Cordova	907-424-7337

Arizona

Purl's II	Tucson	888-37P-URLS
	purlsltd@earthlink.net	

USA stockists continued next page…

USA stockists continued...

California

Navarro River Knits	Ft. Bragg	877-GOT YARN
	www.navarroriverknits.com	
BB's Knits	Santa Barbara	805-569-0531
	bbsknits@aol.com	
In Sheep's Clothing	Davis	530-759-9276
	www.insheepsclothing.com	
Knitting in LaJolla	LaJolla	858-456-4687
The Black Sheep	Encinitas	760-436-9973
Velona's	Anaheim Hills	714-974-1570
	www.velona.com	
Knitropolis	Long Beach	562-856-4566
	www.knitropolis.com	
L'Atelier	Redondo Beach	310-540-4440
L'Atelier	Santa Monica	310-394-4665
In Stitches	Santa Barbara	805-962-9343
	www.institchesyarns.com	
Mendocino Yarn Shop	Mendocino	707-937-0921
	yarnshop@mcn.org	
	www.mendocinoyarnshop.com	
eKnitting.com	Berkeley	800-392-6494
	sarah@eknitting.com	
	www.eknitting.com	
Wildfiber	Santa Monica	310-458-2748
	wildfiber@aol.com	
	www.wildfiber.com	
Uncommon Threads	Los Altos	650-941-1815
Greenwich Yarns	San Francisco	415-567-2535
	www.greenwichyarn.com	
Filati Fine Yarns	Rocklin	800-398-9043
Calistoga Yarns	Calistoga	707-942-5108
Knitting Basket	Oakland	800-654-4887
	kbasket@pacbell.net	
	www.theknittingbasket.com	
The Yarn Place	Capitola	831-476-6480
	www.theyarnplace.com	

Colorado

A Knitted Peace	Littleton	303-730-0366
	www.aknittedpeace.com	

Connecticut

Wool Connection	Avon	800-933-9665
	wool@tiac.net	
	www.woolconnection.com	
Fabric Place	Cromwell	800-336-5744
	www.fabricplace.com	
The Yarn Barn	Woodbridge	203-389-5117
	www.theyarnbarn.com	
Hook n' Needle	Westport	800-960-4404
	www.hook-n-needle.com	

Idaho

Isabel's	Ketchum	208-725-0408
	www.isabelspocket.com	
House of Needlecraft	CoeurD'Alene	888-775-5648

Illinois

Mosaic Yarn Studio	Des Plaines	847-390-1013
	mosaicyarn@aol.com	
Tangled Web Fibers	Oak Park	708-445-8335
	yarn@tangledwebfibers.com	
Fine Line	St. Charles	630-584-9443
	finelineCA@aol.com	
The Weaving Workshop	Chicago	773-929-5776
	weavingworkshop@aol.com	
Nancy's Knitworks	Springfield	800-676-9813
	nanknitwks@aol.com	
We'll Keep You in Stitches	Chicago	312-642-2540

Indiana

Sheep's Clothing	Valparaiso	219-462-4300
Yarns Unlimited	Bloomington	812-334-2464
Mass Ave Knit Shop	Indianapolis	800-675-8565
	www.massaveknitshop.com	

Kansas

Whimsies	Andover	316-733-8881
	whimsiesLPS@aol.com	

Kentucky

Handknitters, Ltd	Louisville	866-468-9276

Maine

Ardith Keef Gifts	Scarborough	207-883-8689
	www.ardithkeef.com	
Stitchery Square	Camden	207-236-9773
	stitchsq@mint.net	
	www.stitching.com/stitcherysquare	
Water Street Yarns	Hallowell	207-622-5500

Maryland

Woolworks	Baltimore	410-337-9030
Yarn Garden of Annapolis	Annapolis	800-738-9276
	www.yarngarden.com	

Massachusettes

Knitting Treasures	Plymouth	508-747-2500
Barehill Studios/Fibre Loft	Harvard	978-456-8669
Knit Witts	Brookfield	1-877-877-knit(5648)
	knitwitts@knitwitts.com	
	www.knitwitts.com	
Northampton Wools	Northampton	413-586-4331
Colorful Stitches	Lenox	800-413-6111
	mary@colorful-stitches.com	
	www.colorful-stitches.com	
Woolcott and Co.	Cambridge	617-547-2837
Wild & Woolly Studio	Lexington Ctr.	781-861-7717
Snow Goose	Milton	617-698-1190
Creative Warehouse	Needham	781-444-9341
	creativewarehse@cs.com	
Ladybug Knitting Shop	Dennis	508-385-2662
	bpldybg@capecod.net	
	www.ladybugknitting.com	
Needle Arts of Concord	Concord	978-371-0424

Michigan

Yarn Quest	Traverse City	231-929-4277
Right Off the Sheep	Birmingham	248-646-7595
The Wool & The Floss	Grosse Pointe	313-882-9110
Threadbender Yarn Shop	Grand Rapids	888-531-6642
Knitting Room	Birmingham	248-540-3623
	www.knittingroom.com	
Whippletree Yarn & Gifts	Hudsonville	616-669-4487
Stitching Memories	Portage	616-552-9276
Yarn for Ewe	Okemos	517-349-9665
The Fibre House	Grand Haven	866-844-2497
	www.forknitters.com	

Minnesota

Linden Hills Yarns	Minneapolis	612-929-1255
A Sheepy Yarn Shoppe	White Bear Lake	800-480-5462
	info@sheepyyarn.com	
	www.sheepyyarnmn.com	
Three Kittens Yarn Shoppe	St. Paul	800-489-4969
Skeins	Minnetonka	952-939-4166
	twistedstitcher@aol.com	
The Yarnery	St. Paul	651-222-5793
Needlework Unlimited	Minneapolis	612-925-2454
	www.needleworkunlimited.com	
Creative Fibers	Minneapolis	612-927-8307
	cfibers@uswest.net	
	www.creativefibers.com	

50

Missouri

Thread Peddler	Springfield	417-886-5404
Hearthstone Knits	St. Louis	314-849-9276
Lynn's Stitchin Tyme	Marshfield	417-859-4494

Montana

Prodigal	Livingston	406-222-6021

Nebraska

Personal Threads Boutique	Omaha	402-391-7733
	www.personalthreads.com	

New Hampshire

The Elegant Ewe	Concord	603-226-0066
	elegantu@worldpass.net	
Charlotte's Web	Exeter	888-244-6460

New Jersey

Accents on Knits	Morristown	973-829-9944
	www.accentsonknits.com	
Hoboken Handknits	Hoboken	201-653-2545
Knitter's Workshop	Garwood	908-789-1333
The Knitting Gallery	Colts Neck	732-294-9276
	www.knittinggallery.com	
The Stitching Bee	Chatham	973-635-6691
	www.thestitchingbee.com	

New Mexico

Village Wools	Albuquerque	800-766-4553
	villagewools@villagewools.com	
	www.villagewools.com	
The Needle's Eye	Santa Fe	800-883-0706

New York

Elegant Needles	Skaneateles	800-275-9276
Garden City Stitches	Garden City	516-739-5648
	www.gardencitystitches.com	
Lee's Yarn Center	Bedford Hills	914-244-3400
	www.leesyarn.com	
Patternworks	Poughkeepsie	800-438-5464
	www.patternworks.com	
Sew Brooklyn	Brooklyn	718-499-7383
The Knitting Connection	East Syracuse	315-445-2911
The Knitting Corner	Huntington	631-421-2660
The Knitting Place, Inc.	Port Washington	516-944-9276
The Woolly Lamb	East Aurora	716-655-1911
The Yarn Connection	New York	212-684-5099
Village Yarn Shop	Rochester	716-454-6064

North Carolina

Great Yarns	Raleigh	800-810-0045
	greatyarn@gte.net	
	www.great-yarns.com	

Ohio

Wolfe Fibre Arts	Columbus	614-487-9980
	www.wolfefiberarts.com	
Fifth Stitch	Defiance	419-782-0991
	alelupp@defnet.com	
	www.fifthstitch.com	
Lambscapes of Ohio	Glendale	513-574-7046
	bforcynthia@juno.com	

Oklahoma

Sealed with a Kiss	Guthrie	405-282-8649
	www.swakknit.com	

Oregon

Woodland Woolworks	Carlton	800-547-3725
	woolwrks@teleport.com	
The Web-sters	Ashland	800-482-9801
	www.yarnatwebsters.com	
Yarn Garden	Portland	503-239-7950
Ann's Yarn Gallery	Tigard	503-684-4851

Pennsylvania

Kathy's Kreations	Ligonier	724-238-9320
	www.kathys-kreations.com	
Mannings Creative	E. Berlin	800-233-7166
	www.the-mannings.com	

Oh Susanna Yarns	Lancaster	717-393-5146
	ohsusannay@aol.com	
Wool Gathering	Kennett Square	610-444-8236
	knit@woolgathering.com	

Rhode Island

A Stitch Above	Providence	800-949-5648
	natalie@astitchaboveknitting.com	
	www.astitchaboveknitting.com	
Sakonnet Purls	Tiverton	888-624-9902
	sakpurls@worldnet.att.net	
	www.sakonnetpurls.com	

Tennesee

Angel Hair Yarns	Nashville	615-269-8833
	www.angelhairyarn.com	
Genuine Purl Too	Chattanooga	423-267-7335

Texas

Needleart	Spring	281-288-4881
	www.needleart.net	
Woolie Ewe	Plano	972-424-3163
	www.wooliewe.com	
Turrentines	Houston	713-661-9411
	nanknit@swbell.net	
Yarn Barn of San Antonio	San Antonio	210-826-3679

Utah

Needlepoint Joint	Ogden	801-394-4355
	www.needlepointjoint.com	

Virginia

Hunt Country Yarns	Middleburg	540-687-5129
	www.skeins.com	
Aylin's Woolgatherer	Falls Church	703-573-1900
	www.aylinswoolgatherer.com	
Old Town Needlecrafts	Manassas	703-330-1846
Knitting Basket Ltd	Richmond	804-282-2909
Orchardside Yarn Shop	Raphine	540-348-5220
	www.oysyarnshop.com	
The Knitting Corner, Inc.	Virginia Beach	757-420-7547
	theknitcorner@aol.com	
	www.theknittingcorner.com	
On Pins & Needles	Toano	800-484-5191 ext. 9334
	onpins&needles.html	
	www.widowmaker.com/~vcdavis	
Got Yarn	Richmond	888-242-4474
	yarnqueen@gotyarn.com	
	www.gotyarn.com	

Washington

Banana Belt Yarns	Sequim	360-683-5852
Churchmouse Yarns & Teas	Bainbridge Island	206-780-2686
	kit@churchmouse.com	
	www.churchmouseyarns.com	
The Weaving Works	Seattle	888-524-1221
	weavingworks@earthlink.net	
	www.weavingworks.com	
Tricoter	Seattle	206-328-6505
Wild & Wooly Yarn Co.	Poulsbo	800-743-2100
Skeins Ltd	Bellevue	425-452-1248
Amanda's Yarns	Poulsbo	360-779-3666
	yarnstore@silverlink.net	
	www.yarntoknit.com	

Wisconsin

Jane's Knitting Hutch	Appleton	920-954-9001
	www.angelfire.com/biz2/yarnshop/index.html	
Easy Stitchin' Needleart, Inc.	Sister Bay	920-854-2840
Ruhama's Yarn & Needlepoint	Milwaukee	414-332-2660
	dawnann@gte.net	
Herrschners Inc.	Stevens Point	800-713-1239
	www.herrschners.com	
Lakeside Fibers	Madison	608-257-2999
	susanh@lakesidefibers.com	
	www.lakesidefibers.com	

JO SHARP

Information about Jo Sharp yarn and caring for your garment

Investment Knitting

With care, the Jo Sharp garment you create this year will become a trusted favourite for years to come. Spun from premium grade, long fibre fleece, Jo Sharp yarn knits into a hard-wearing item of clothing that is beautifully warm and soft. It is not surprising that our wool performs so well when you consider it has survived all the elements while still on the sheep's back. Pure wool is practical, long-lasting and natural. A Jo Sharp wool garment will stand up to harsh outdoor conditions whilst keeping its softness and good looks throughout years of wear. Wool knitwear requires care and attention when it is washed, however it does not soil easily and requires maintenance less frequently than other fibres. Wool is truly a noble fibre!

Not machine wash treated

Jo Sharp Hand Knitting Yarn has a natural crimp and elasticity which makes it satisfying to knit with. Its waxy outer coating of tiny overlapping scales (rather like roof shingles), repel liquids and particles of dust or dirt. Wool contains millions of tiny pockets of air which act as natural thermal insulators. Unfortunately, machine wash treatment puts an artificial resin coating on wool fibres, effectively gluing them together and damaging their natural thermal characteristics. This treatment also gives wool yarn an un-natural shiny appearance. For these reasons, we chose not to treat our yarn with the machine wash process.

Less Pilling

Inferior short fibres (which can cause pilling and itching) are removed during processing of Jo Sharp yarn. This treatment improves the yarn's natural softness and wash and wear performance. With care, your quality Jo Sharp garment will improve with age and wear.

Combing

When our extra long fibre yarn is processed, most of the short fibres are removed. If, in the first few weeks of wear, a few remaining short fibres shed, causing a small amount of pilling, these pills should be combed from your garment using a "de-piller" comb. De-pilling combs are generally inexpensive and are available from craft and knitting stores.

What causes wool knitwear to shrink?

Nature designed wool fibres to be a protective coating for sheep in all weather. The unique outer scale structure of the wool fibre resists soiling, but is also the reason why wool shrinks when not cared for properly. With severe agitation or tumble drying, the scales on the fibre lock together causing the garment to reduce in size and become thick and fluffy (felted). If you carefully follow the washing instructions on the inside of the Jo Sharp yarn label or at right, you should not encounter any problems with shrinkage.

Hand Washing

For the best result, turn garment inside out and gently hand wash in lukewarm water, using a wool detergent. Rinse thoroughly in lukewarm water. Rinse again in cold water.

Drying

To remove excess moisture after washing, roll garment inside a large towel and gently squeeze, alternatively, spin dry inside a pillow case. Never tumble dry. Place garment on a flat surface in the shade to dry, coaxing it back into shape whilst damp. Drying flat is recommended. Do not dry directly in front of an open or artificial fire.

Dry cleaning

Generally is not recommended as residual dry cleaning chemicals tend to harden wool fabric.

Yarn Specification

Jo Sharp 8ply DK Pure Wool hand knitting yarn is made from extra fine and soft 100% Merino/Border Leicester fleece.
(DK is the USA and UK equivalent of Australian 8 ply)
One Ball of yarn is approximately 50g (1 3/4 oz)
and 98 Mtrs (107 yards) in length.
Tension/Gauge:
Stocking stitch / 22.5 sts and 30 rows.
Measured over 10cm (approx. 4").
Using 4.00mm (USA 6) (UK 8) needles.